THE ECONOMY IS SPINNING

Edited by Kris Dittel

ONOMATOPEE 132

I NEVER READ THE ECONOMIST.

TABLE OF CONTENT

Jan Hoeft
EXIT STRATEGIES
6

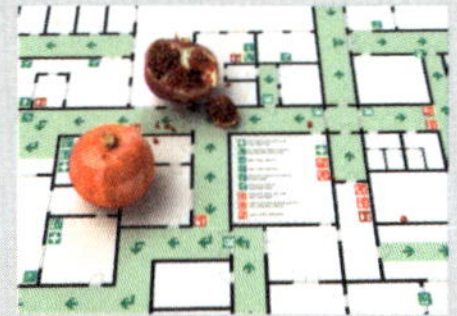

Kris Dittel
INTRODUCTION
10

Mercedes Azpilicueta
GEOMETRIC DANCER
DOESN'T BELIEVE IN LOVE,
FINDS ASPIRATION AND
ECSTASY IN SPIRALS
18

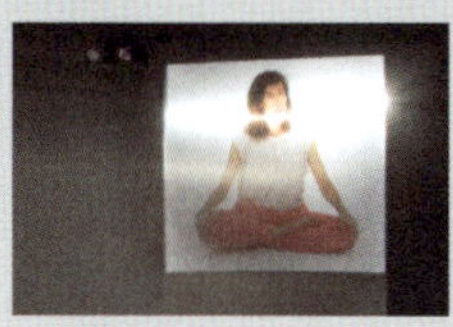

Sara Giannini
YOU HAVE MY WORD
NOTES ON WORDS,
MONEY AND GOD
20

Monique Hendriksen
DELUSIONAL CAUSE
38

ON NATURE
42

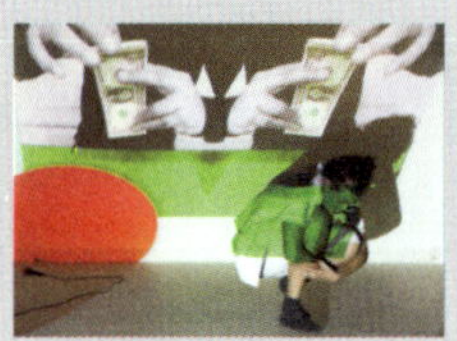

Sami Khatib
UNDEAD LABOUR
UN/SPINNING THE TIME
OF REAL ABSTRACTION
48

Zachary Formwalt
KRITIK DER POLITIK UND
NATIONALÖKONOMIE
60

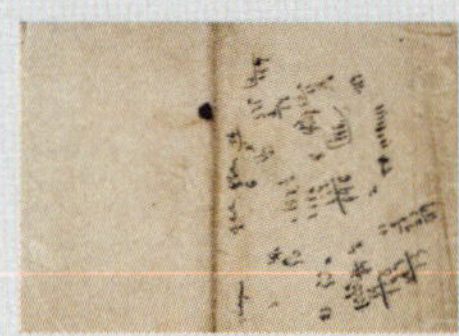

Antonis Pittas
ON COLOUR THEORY
80

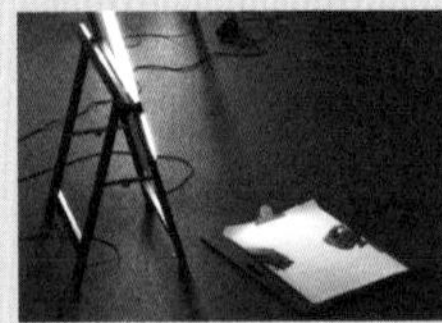

McKenzie Wark
THE SUBLIME LANGUAGE
OF MY CENTURY
88

Nick Thurston
STATUS_ANXIETIES
102

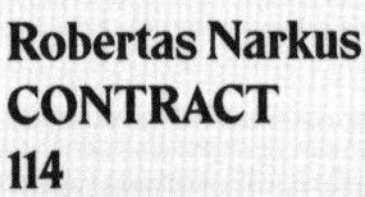

Robertas Narkus
CONTRACT
114

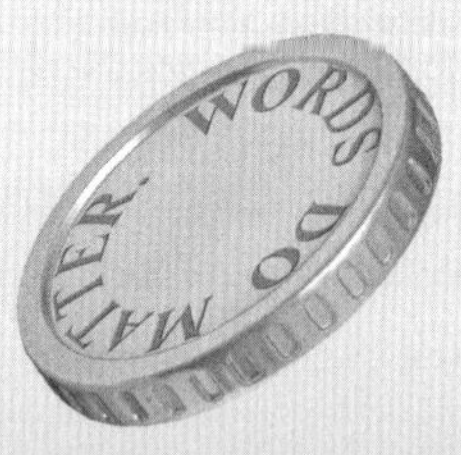

Hanne Lippard
I AM MRS HELEN WONG,
WE NEED TO DISCUSS
AS PROMISED
27, 47, 86–87, 116, 149–150

EXHIBITION
DOCUMENTATION
116

EPILOGUE
151

BIOGRAPHIES OF
CONTRIBUTORS
152

INDEX DETOUR
154

LIST OF WORKS IN
THE EXHIBITION
156

COLOPHON
158

FOLLOWING PAGES

Jan Hoeft
EXIT STRATEGIES

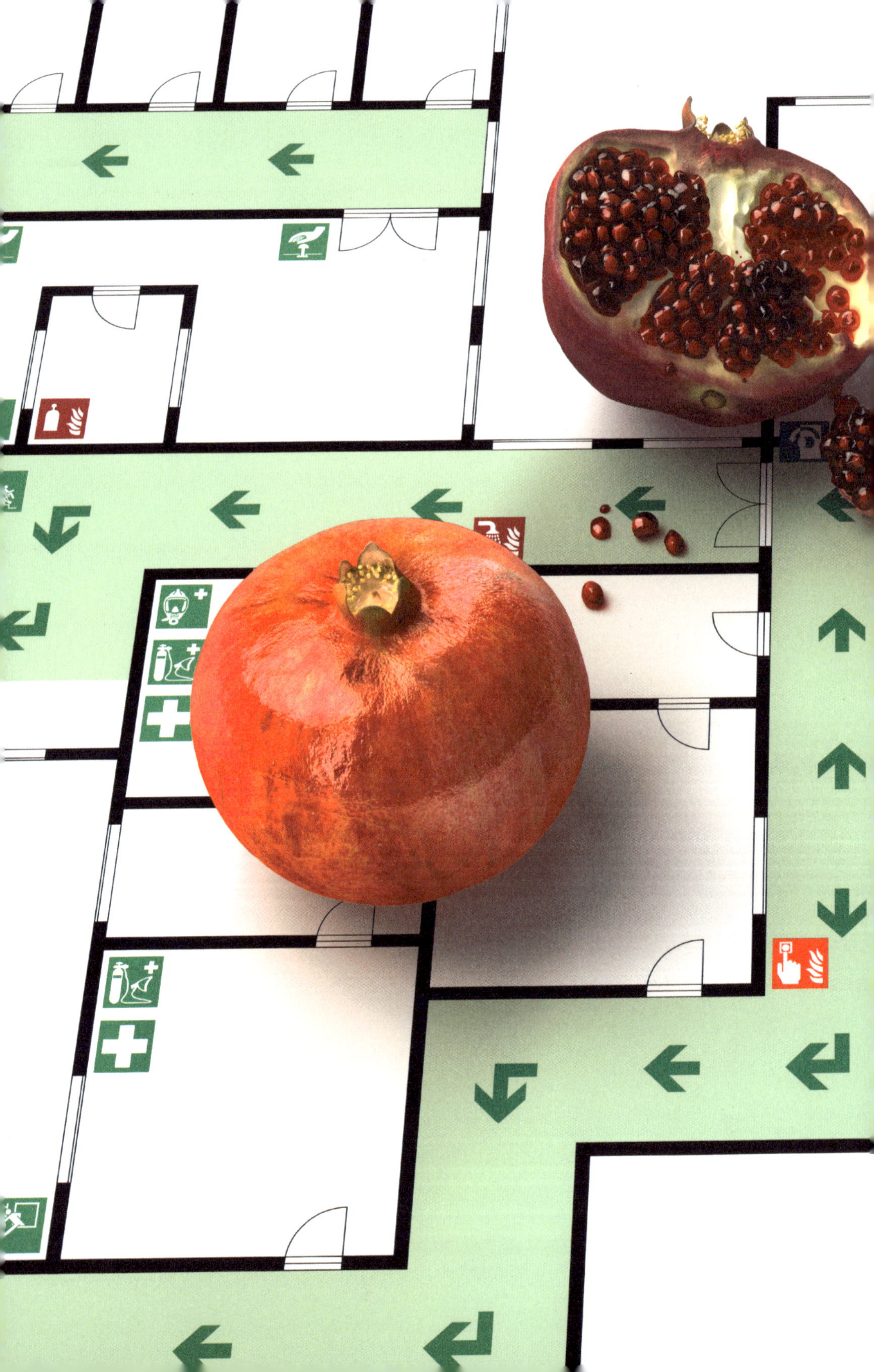

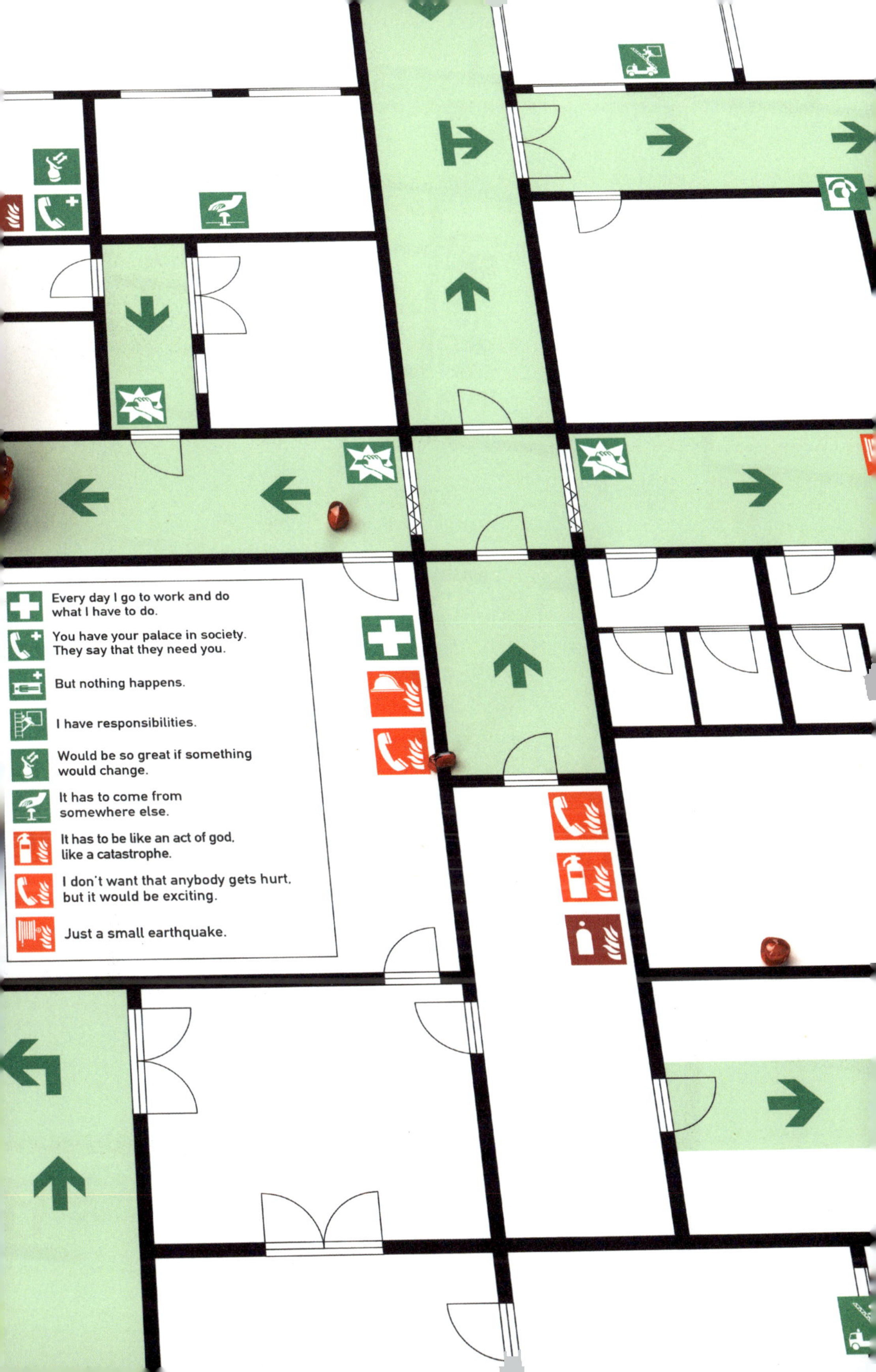
Every day I go to work and do what I have to do.
You have your palace in society. They say that they need you.
But nothing happens.
I have responsibilities.
Would be so great if something would change.
It has to come from somewhere else.
It has to be like an act of god, like a catastrophe.
I don't want that anybody gets hurt, but it would be exciting.
Just a small earthquake.

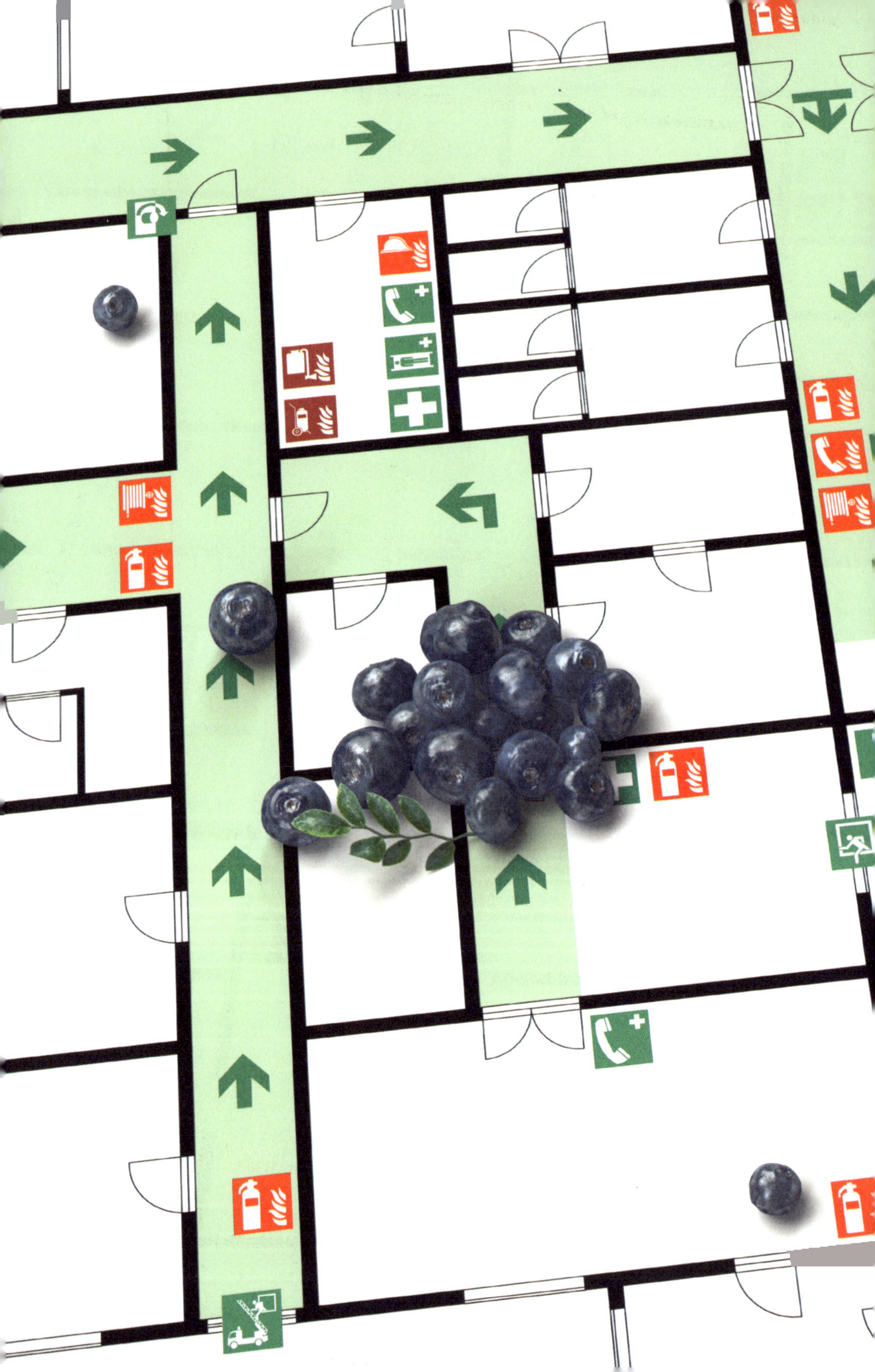

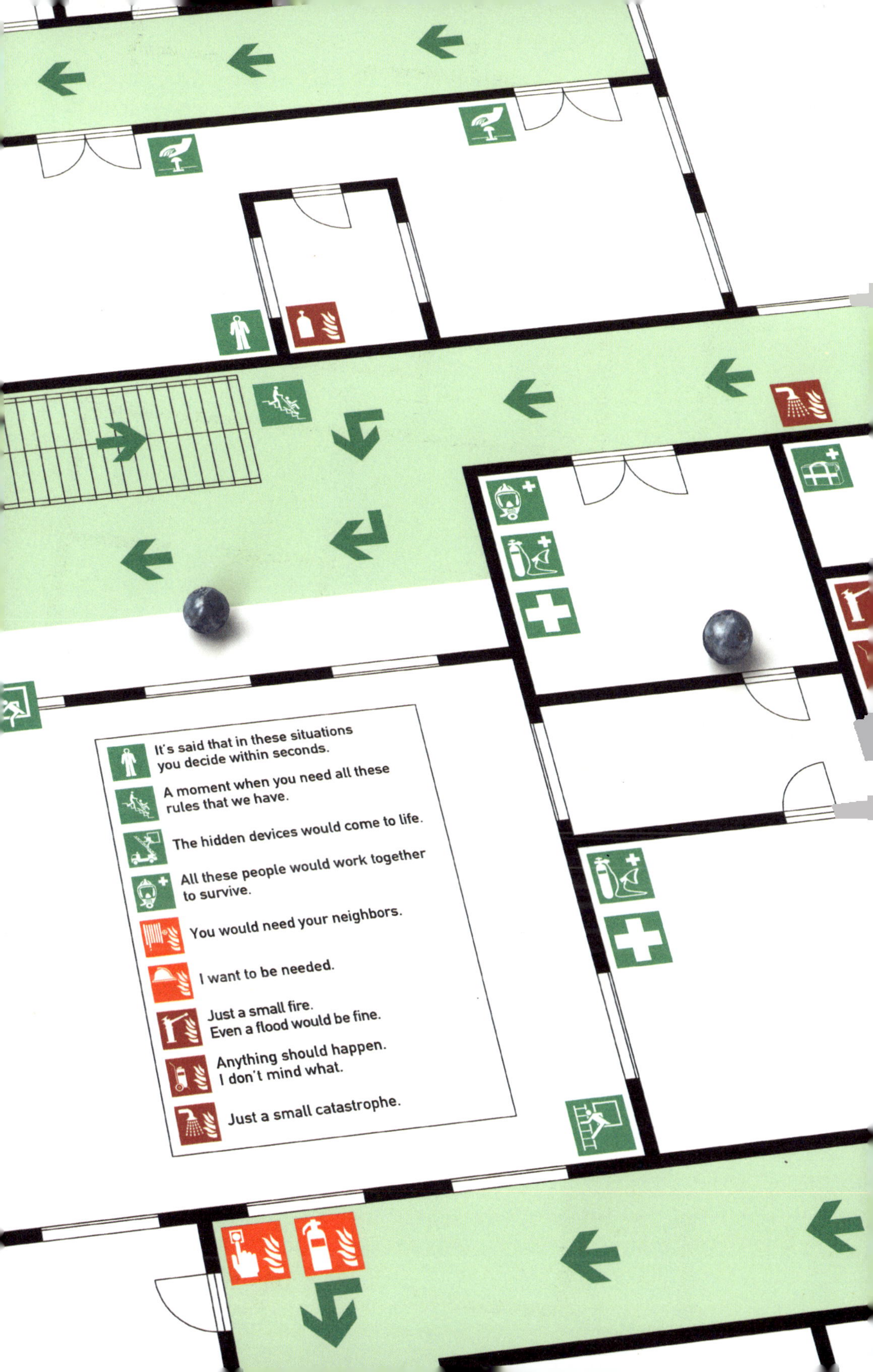

It's said that in these situations
you decide within seconds.

A moment when you need all these
rules that we have.

The hidden devices would come to life.

All these people would work together
to survive.

You would need your neighbors.

I want to be needed.

Just a small fire.
Even a flood would be fine.

Anything should happen.
I don't mind what.

Just a small catastrophe.

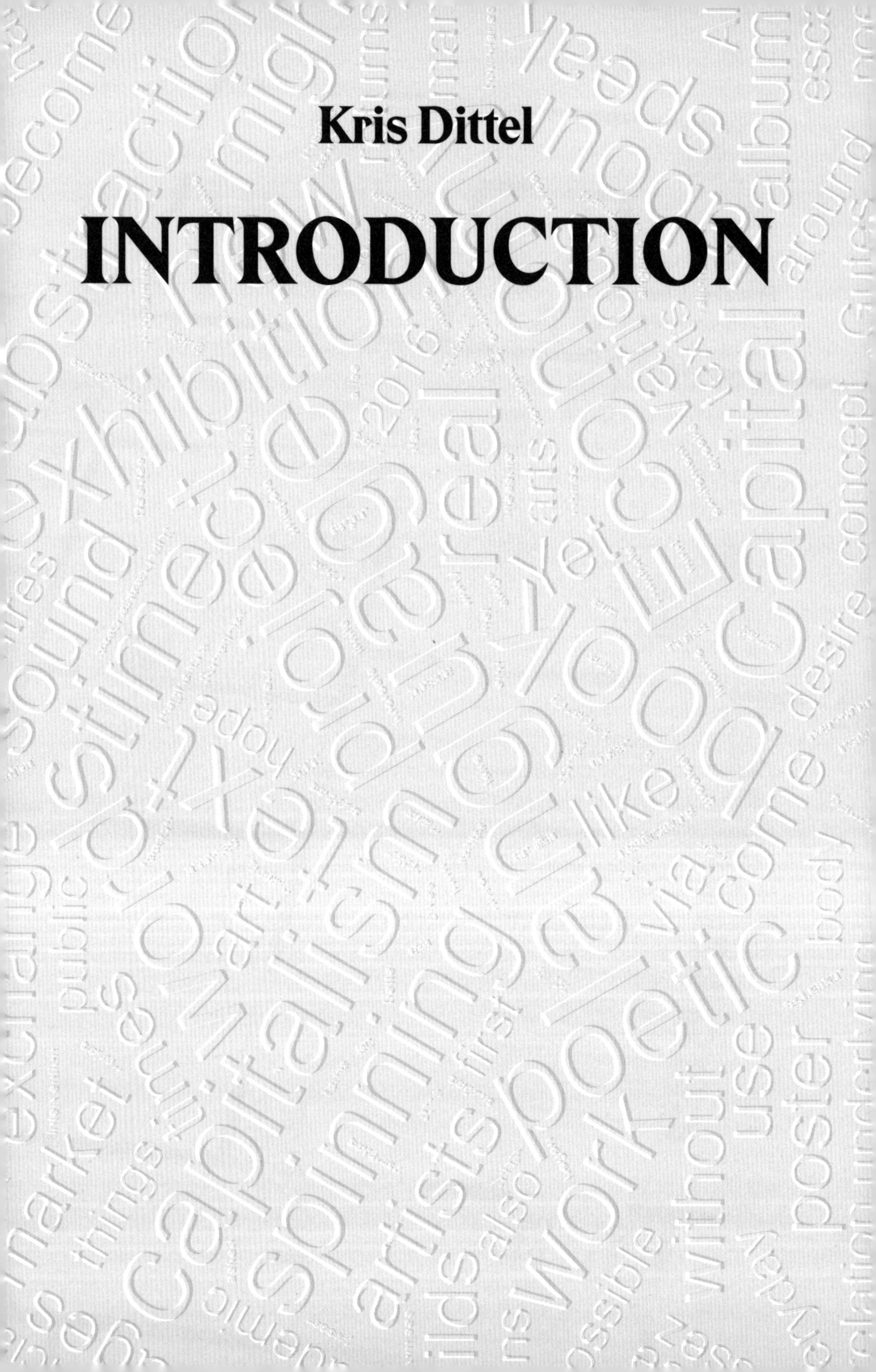

INTRODUCTION

How does the economy speak to us? Does it speak through us? Sometimes its voice trembles with fear, and at other times it whispers with hope and sings in excitement about better days to come.

Economic jargon settles in and makes things sound correct by making them sound familiar; it comes to our aid when troubles arise and comforts us with its reasonable-sounding justifications. Like religion, it gives hope and solace, soothes worry and anguish. This doctrine is everywhere. It oozes out of academic studies and financial newspapers. "Efficiency" has become the measure of the everyday, as "cost-benefit analyses" guide us to make decisions in the interests of the greatest possible returns. This logic promises freedom in exchange for leaving things to take their own course: laissez faire, laissez passer. The "invisible hand" of the market should ensure that needs and wants are met without any outside intervention or regulation, yet needs and wants are not governed by rational rules; the desire to have it all, to have it now and without limits, is a notion without end, with irrationality as its command.[1]

The Economy is Spinning began as an exhibition project and public programme that looked into various manifestations of the language of economics and finance, a language that permeates our vocabularies and builds the boundaries of our imaginations. The project considered the economy to be a "performing body", a body that speaks, and asked what its language might reveal about its frame of mind. With contributions by nine artists, the exhibition aimed to accentuate and exaggerate the absurdity of this language and of its underlying ideological mechanisms.

This publication brings together contributions from artists who participated in the exhibition with those from invited writers to form an extension of the initial project. Besides examining the mechanisms and modes of performance of economic mantras, this book attempts to manifest poetic

1 "Reason is always a region cut out of the irrational", or so say D&G, "a region traversed by the irrational. Underneath all reasons lies delirium, drift. Everything is rational in capitalism, except capital or capitalism itself. The stock market is certainly rational; one can understand it, study it, the capitalists know how to use it, and yet it is completely delirious, it's mad. It is in this sense that we say: the rational is always the rationality of an irrational." (Gilles Deleuze and Félix Guattari, *Chaosophy*, ed. Sylvère Lotringer, Autonomedia/ Semiotexte, 1995).

counter-expressions via art and theory alike. The artists'
contributions are reassembled here in a new constellation
around three texts that also mark three distinct points of
interest: the relations between religious language and the
mantras of capitalism; the concept of the real abstraction of
capital, and its relevance to time; and a call to reinvent and
reform our vocabularies and thinking around new visions
and realities.

The opening pages of this book accommodate modified
evacuation plans by Jan Hoeft. Instead of providing safety
instructions, these plans speak of a desire for a catastrophe.
Their layouts seem characteristic of the symbols of today's
centres of power and capital, as they are seen in Hoeft's film,
Exit Strategies. These centres of capital require the 24/7
presence of labour, and offer catastrophe as the only possible
method of escape.

*Geometric Dancer Doesn't Believe in Love, Finds Aspiration
and Ecstasy in Spirals* is the script of Mercedes Azpilicueta's
work of the same name, a two-channel video installation.
The work is a vocal re-iteration of sound fragments that
were recorded at sites of trade in the port city of Rotterdam
—the street, the market, the harbour—yet which might have
been recorded at any other centre of capital. The drawings
included in this book are visual mnemonics produced via a
personal encoding system that translates the soundscapes
into visual poetry.

Sara Giannini's text takes its readers through a genealogy of the
language of capitalism to its historical and structural source
in Christianity.[2] The essay traces the development of this
language back to the mythical moment of separation between
the divine and human languages—the Fall from Paradise—
after which humankind found itself among a cacophony of
noises (in Babel), and language became a slippery tool—
convertible, liquid and transactional in its nature. Perhaps
language is the new liquidity of the (near) future.

2 Walter Benjamin
writes in his unfinished
essay *Capitalism as
Religion* about the
religious structure
of capitalism and the
appropriations of
religious concepts
such as guilt/debt
[Schuld]: Capitalism
is presumably
the first case of
aculpabilizing/indebting
[verschuldend], rather
than repenting/de-
atoning cult. Herein
stands this religious
system in the fall of a
tremendous movement.
An enormous feeling
of guilt/debt [Schuld]
not itself knowing how
to repent/de-atone,
grasps at the cult, not
in order to repent for
this guilt, but to make
it universal, to hammer
it into consciousness
and finally and above all
to include God himself
in this guilt, in order to
finally interest him in
repentance.

Monique Hendriksen's contribution starts with the poetic script of her performance *Delusional Cause*. Her research, which is centred on the question of how to visualize and represent capital, is formulated in a secondary text, *On Nature*, which builds on Alfred Sohn-Rethel's work on the real abstraction of commodity exchange.[3] This text lays out the basic concepts for a speculative exploration of capital's real abstraction and aesthetics in an era when capital has become impenetrably complex.

Sami Khatib's text *Undead Labour – Un/Spinning the Time of Real Abstraction* builds upon the work of Alfred Sohn-Rethel, in which Kant's epistemology is combined with Marx's critique of political economy. As he guides us through the concepts of real abstraction[3], abstract human labour, and commodity abstraction, Khatib pays special attention to their relationships with the concept of time, a dominant social relation in capitalism. "Time is money!", declares the capitalist, before transforming the bearers of labour power into undead zombie creatures—creatures "whose commodified agency returns to the surface of the market."

Zachary Formwalt's text *Schäuble and the Critique of Political Economy* is composed of personal notes relating to the exhibition *Gutes Böses Geld*, which was held at the Kunsthalle Baden-Baden in 2016. The situation surrounding this exhibition, particularly with regard to the German financial minister Wolfgang Schäuble's patronage of the project, was the impetus for this contribution. Formwalt's text addresses the operation of private and public sponsorship in the arts, the use of art as a blanket apparatus for political propaganda, and the question of art's agency in such circumstances. Formwalt quotes an introductory text authored by Schäuble himself, in which the terms "neoliberal", "wisdom" and "prudence" become interchangeable. Formwalt's work *Kritik der Politik und Nationalökonomie* was simultaneously on display in both *Gutes Böses Geld* and *The Economy is Spinning*.

3 Abstraction is usually treated as unique to human condition, but for Sohn-Rehel, in *Intellectual and Manual Labour*, abstraction takes place in the "real". Sohn-Rethel proposed that this "real abstraction" can happen outside of and before the human mind's abstraction. In fact, commodity exchange is such a "real abstraction." "The essence of commodity abstraction, however, is that it is not thought-induced; it does not originate in men's minds but in their actions. And yet this does not give 'abstraction' a merely metaphorical meaning. It is abstraction in its precise, literal sense. [...] While the concepts of natural science are thought abstractions, the economic concept of value is a real one. It exists nowhere other than in the human mind but it does not spring from it. Rather it is purely social in character, arising in the spatio-temporal sphere of human interrelations. It is not people who originate these abstractions but their actions. 'They do this without being aware of it.' "(Alfred Sohn-Rethel, *Intellectual and Manual Labour. A Critique of Epistemology*, London: Macmillan, 1978, p. 20).

A six-page image sequence by the artist Antonis Pittas
draws on the archive of Gustav Klutsis, a core member of
the Russian Constructivist movement. Klutsis' broadcasting
towers and mobile poster stands spoke the language of
revolution and functioned as propaganda tools. Pittas, whose
long-term research deals with the relation between the avant-
garde and European politics, gradually covers the original
image in this sequence, creating a choreography of the hand
to re-perform its legacy. The "artist's hands" signal a gesture
of new times to come, times in which a new faith is to be built
and a new language created.

Capitalism is a strange word; it describes a system that has
completely rendered our world to the extent that it is hard
to grasp any concepts or definitions beyond it. McKenzie
Wark proposes a thought experiment that might sound like
science fiction but feels too close to reality all the same. We
like to think that once capitalism is overturned, once it has
eaten itself, its doomsday will be followed by a *tabula rasa*,
a new beginning. Yet Wark predicts that what will come
after capitalism might be something even worse. This new
infrastructure might commodify everything, transforming it
into information, until there's no more of this world/word left.

Of the Subcontract, Or Principles of Poetic Right, a book
project (2013) by Nick Thurston, is comprised of a collection
of poems about computational capitalism. The poems
of *Of the Subcontract* were commissioned via Amazon's
Mechanical Turk service and written by its workers, who
perform customized tasks for minimum payment. *Of the
Subcontract* reduces the poetic imagination to exploited
labour and elevates "artificial artificial" intelligence to the
status of the poetic. The book was translated into Dutch for
The Economy is Spinning (as *Van de onderaanneming of,
Principles of Poetic Right*) and was available as a print-on-
demand publication throughout the duration of the exhibition.
In the text published here, *Status_Anxieties*, Thurston
outlines his account of his project, followed by a few pages
copied from the Dutch version of the poetry book.

Robertas Narkus' contribution is a transcript of the words spoken by Martin Shkreli in a YouTube video addressed to Wu-Tang. Shkreli became "the most hated man in the World" and the "poster child of greed" after, as a hedge fund founder and the CEO of a pharmaceutical firm, he acquired the rights to a widely used medicine and raised its price by 5000 per cent overnight. In 2015, the "most hated man" bought the "most exclusive rap album of all time": the single existing copy of the Wu-Tang Clan album *Once Upon a Time in Shaolin*. Wu-Tang imposed a commercial ban on the release of any more copies, further mystifying the album. The text echoes a Faustian pact with the devil—the exchange of diabolical favours for money in this case.

Hanne Lippard's fictional character, Mrs Helen Wong, intrudes upon the structure of the book with an array of unsolicited messages in the language of a spambot (*I am Mrs Helen Wong, we need to discuss as promised*). Helen Wong addresses us and conceals her message behind the language of the everyday. She hides her real demands and desires in an attempt to seep through the spam filters that decide which messages may penetrate inboxes freely. Do spambots speak the unconscious language of the Internet?[4]

A poster by Toril Johannessen, titled *Balance in Economy and Ecology*, supplements the book. The work is part of her ongoing series, *Words and Years*, which charts the use over time of particular words in various academic journals and news magazines. Going through the complete volumes of these journals from their first issues up to the present day, the frequency of the use of selected words is mapped. The strangely poetic diagrams that result raise questions regarding the motivations underlying scientific enquiry, and their graphic representation.

The last chapter of the book is composed of images of the exhibition *The Economy is Spinning*, which took place between June 9 and July 17, 2016 at Onomatopee, Eindhoven.

4 In Sandy Baldwin's book *The Internet Unconscious: On the Subject of Electronic Literature* I read about how spam filters gradually learn which words are being used for user communications and which indicate that a message is spam. As the machine learns, it filters through all the words and renders the probability of a text being spam in relation to all other spams. Baldwin writes: "As a result, all text is probable spam as a condition of its communicability. All text is an amalgam of spam and communication. The intention of a text, one directed to me and that I desire to read, is always partially spam. The political economy underlying spam renders the text as product, and renders my rendering of the spam as a medium or interface to consumption. In this sense, spam is a perfect model of the communication circuit, of the message received."

Finally, a few words on some design elements of the book. The coins that appear throughout the book were developed by the book's graphic designer, Rafaela Dražić, and their short slogans were sourced from economic journals, newspapers, advertisement campaigns, and in some cases from the surrounding texts.

Inspiration for the chart-like visualizations that run across the book's cover and those pages containing photographs from the exhibition was drawn from various sources, including: economic graphs representing interest rates, effects of bank regulations, commodity futures prices, etc.; the lines of city skylines overgrown with skyscrapers; and finally, from a subjective model developed in order to produce graphical representations of dreams. The resulting design, in which charts and skylines grow into dreamscapes, in a way also refers to the origin of the title of this project: "The Economy is Spinning" was first uttered in a moment of dreamspeak, in a state between sleep and wakefulness, as if it was itself produced by the capitalist unconscious.

It is seemingly impossible to escape the all-swallowing mechanisms of capitalism; the performance of its spinning wheel never stops. Capital flows, and fluctuates as wealth, commodity, art, and language. Perhaps someday, when words themselves are commodified, when their utterance is the production of nothing more than surplus-value, we will have eventually talked words into meaninglessness. Until then, there's still an opportunity for poetic language to entangle and resist the spinning wheel of capitalism. After all, words do matter.

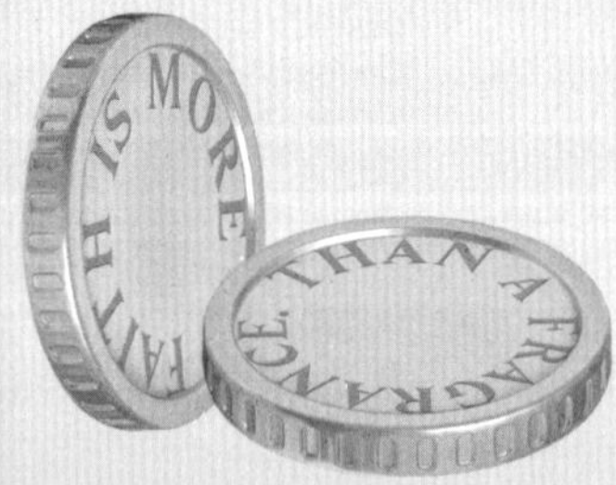

FOLLOWING PAGES

→

Mercedes Azpilicueta
**GEOMETRIC DANCER DOESN'T BELIEVE IN LOVE,
FINDS ASPIRATION AND ECSTASY IN SPIRALS**

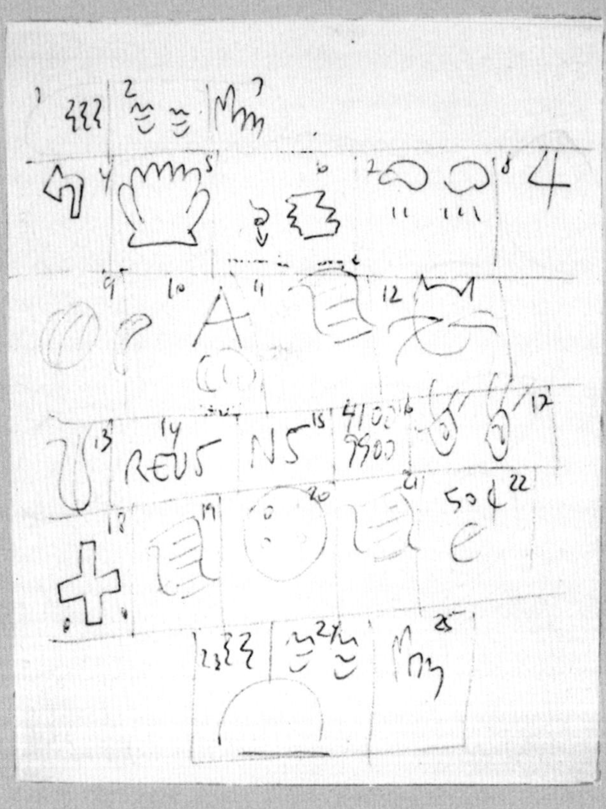

Geometric Dancer

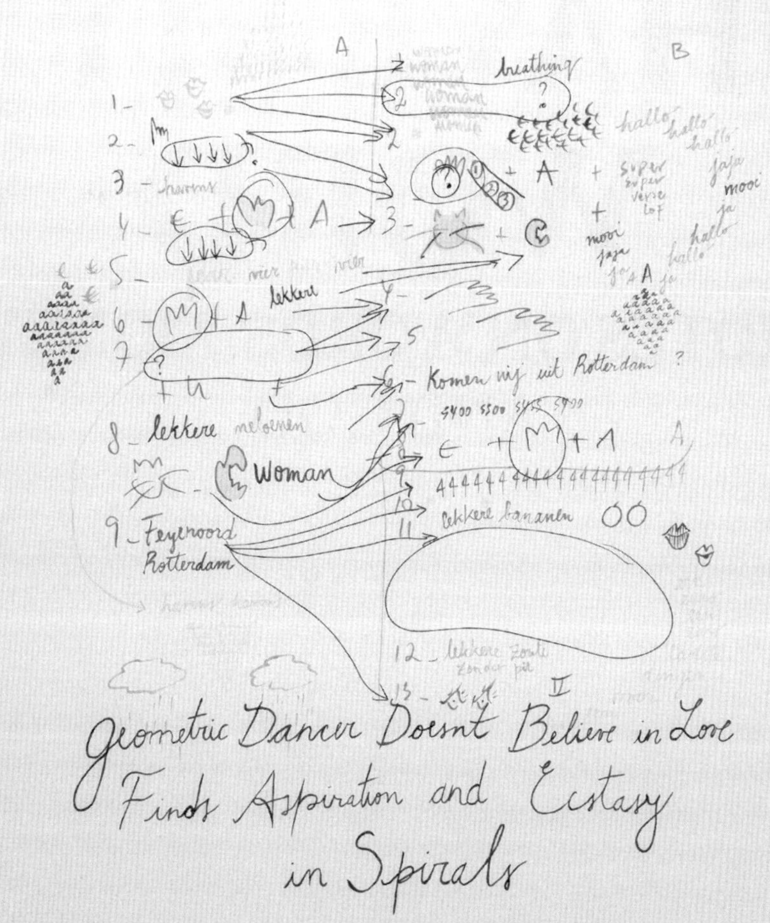

Geometric Dancer Doesn't Believe in Love

Finds Aspiration and Ecstasy

in Spirals

Sara Giannini

YOU HAVE MY WORD

NOTES ON WORDS, MONEY AND GOD

The following essay is an attempt to trace the interweaving of words, money and divine matter (pardon the oxymoron) throughout the history and mythology of Capitalism.

An allusion:
If God is Word, and Money is God, is Word Money?

A word of warning:
I grew up in Italy in a "Catho-Communist" family (a widespread entity in that part of the world). I trust then that you will understand if this text is punctuated by references to both the Bible and (post-)Marxist theory.

I
IN THE BEGINNING WAS THE WORD

In the beginning was the Word,
and the Word was with God,
and the Word was God.
He was with God in the beginning.

For quite a long time I believed in the tale of Adam and Eve living happily and naked in the Garden of Eden. But sadly, just like them, at some point I lost my innocence, and it now seems to me that the Book of Genesis is nothing other than a saga of semiotic traumas.

According to the Holy Scriptures, the creation of the world is *via* the Word—which is God—which is the Word. This equation may perhaps become clearer when we consider the ancient Greek *logos*, a polysemic concept indicating thinking, language, and the order/origin of knowledge.

In being the Word, God is a non-semiotic unity. That is to say: a language where no semiosis subsists; an eternal, immutable and paradigmatic text; a language of identity which is neither differential nor referential.

Creation is purely a linguistic performance. At God's every utterance something appears:

And God said, "Let there be light"; and there was light.
—(Genesis 1:3, ESV)

As the story goes, God creates Adam after creating all the other earthly creatures and grants him the power to name them. Unfortunately, however, poor Adam is not God and naming is not enough for him. Surely it is not creational.[1]

While God can produce and reproduce itself through language, the fleshy Adam needs another body in order to do so. And it is because humans cannot reproduce via self-fulfilling language alone that the vicious Eve makes her debut in Paradise. Human reproduction is exteriorised and thus becomes relational, like human language. (That part wasn't so bad for us after all; words are fun, but sex is better.)

Despite this slight difference—humanity's need for sex—it's said that it was in the image of God that Adam was created. The language spoken by Adam, known as Adamic or Paradisiac Language, was allegedly greatly similar to the divine tongue of God, and for centuries the two were believed to be the same pure language. In this language, names and things live in total harmony: things perfectly adhere to their names and names perfectly adhere to their things; there is no separation between signifier and signified. For Walter Benjamin, this characteristic of the Adamic language represents the short-lived "communion of man with the creative word of God." (Benjamin, 1916: 69)

At the moment of the original, epistemic sin, that communion is broken. Human language is condemned to eternal semiosis, and the poor couple, now aware of their naked misery, are expelled from Paradise. The drama of language and time—in one word, *history*—could finally begin. And with the introduction of historical time language began to mutate, to lose its divine unity and immutability.

Understanding the intimacy between time and language is essential to understanding the intimacy between language and the economy: time produces change, change produces difference, difference creates value. (Remember? Time is money!) Via time, language becomes opaque, relational and transactional, and in

[1] "Now out of the ground the LORD God had formed every beast of the field and every bird of the heavens and brought them to the man to see what he would call them. And whatever the man called every living creature, that was its name. The man gave names to all livestock and to the birds of the heavens and to every beast of the field. But for Adam there was not found a helper fit for him."
—(Genesis 2:20, ESV)

doing so assumes its first economic traits. Signification is the essence of "commodity language," a language of promise and referral in which names are unhooked from (and in constant search of) their referents.

A progressive separation between divine and human language is accounted for by the series of semiotic revenges that begins with The Fall and continues with the Tower of Babel. In this second episode, God, in order to punish men for their ambition and curiosity, multiplies the number of their languages so that they can no longer understand each other. Having inflicting signification on humans with The Fall, God here complicates the task of semiosis. Human language and communication become matters of interpretation, translation and relation—not only among names and things, but also among loose signifiers and the signified. After Babel, human language achieves a fully "transactional" profile, where words and meanings can be converted, exchanged and traded between different tongues.[2]

> [2] For more on this topic see George Steiner, 1975, *After Babel: Aspects of Language and Translation*, Oxford University Press.

II
"THOU SHALT HAVE NO OTHER GODS BEFORE ME"

As is often the case for those stuck in serious long-term relationships, God is (and has always been) an extremely jealous partner:

Do not follow other gods, the gods of the peoples around you; for Yahweh, your God, is a jealous God and His anger will burn against you, and He will destroy you from the face of the land.
—(Deuteronomy 6:15, NIV)

God was terribly afraid (or aware?) that "other gods" would one day take its place. But who are these feared enemies?

The Bible suggests that God's pagan competitors are nothing but personifications of money and wealth. Both the Old and the New Testament repetitively warn humans against the false promise of material possessions and the worship of idols and deities, which are themselves material, visual reproductions of some invisible divine ideal (a state of affairs which resonates with the Platonic theory of forms).

The Book of Exodus provides the first straightforward
comparison between money and other gods. Here the appearance
and subsequent prohibition of the false idol of the Golden
Calf intersects with the establishment of monotheism through
God's proper name. We are told that at the burning bush on
Mount Sinai God reveals its name to Moses for the first time,
identifying itself as the same God that had been encountered
by Moses' ancestors:

*Thus you will say to Israel's sons: "Yahweh your fathers' deity,
Abraham's deity, Isaac's deity, and Jacob's deity—He has sent me
to you;" This is My name to eternity, and this is My designation
age (by) age. (Exodus 3:15, Anchor Bible)*

God discloses its linguistic immutability in order to establish
on earth its own perpetual law, the Ten Commandments.
The catechism of the Catholic Church affirms that the first
commandment, "Thou shalt have no other gods before me,"
forbids honouring gods other than the one who has revealed his
name to his people.

However, humans are damned by the very structure of language
to fail to meet the precepts of monotheism, and to look for
other shelters. This damnation is a result of the disembodied
relationship between names and referents, between signifiers
and signifieds. Our words are actually always signs for other
things. Humans constantly need to see, touch and have in order
to counterbalance the arbitrariness of language. Materiality,
possession and primitive accumulation are what mark both the
recurrent betrayal of God and the history of capitalism.

In fact, it was during Moses' long absence on Mount Sinai
that the people of Israel lost faith in the "only-words God"
and decided to forge instead a new, shiny, always-present idol:
the golden calf. In contrast with the stable yet impalpable Word
of God, the golden calf represents a moral system based upon
the worldly categories of power, beauty, and the works of our
own hands. To put it simply: the economy. It goes without
saying that the first commandment was being broken even as
it was proclaimed.

III
THE WORD BECAME FLESH

In the Christian tradition, it is through a linguistic miracle that God decides to save humans from themselves and to liberate them from disbelief. God incarnates this in his beloved son Jesus:

The Word became flesh and made His dwelling among us.
—(John 1:14, NIV)

Jesus constitutes the redemptive reunion of name and thing, of signifier and signified, sent from the father to renew the broken alliance between mortals and God. In his materiality, Jesus is semantically pregnant. He is true man and true god. He is full truth: the bodily promise of semiotic universal peace.

With the incarnation of the word, the New Testament confirms and emphasises the apparent incompatibility of monotheism and capitalism. "You cannot serve both God and money", preached Jesus, for they are two mutually exclusive systems of belief, one based on the *word* and the other on the *world* (Matthew 6: 24). The love of money becomes "the root of all kinds of evil" (Timothy 6:10, King James Bible) and should therefore be fiercely feared and eradicated, while the pagan gods of the Old Testament are reimagined as Satan and his temptations.

During his famous visit to the temple in Jerusalem, Jesus furiously kicks out the crowd of merchants and moneychangers filling its courtyard, telling them:

My house shall be called the house of prayer; but ye have made it a den of thieves. —(Matthew 21:13, King James Bible)

It is quite revealing that merchants are "thieves" in the eyes of God/Jesus: perhaps thieves of faith? Nevertheless, as we shall see, the advent of capitalism is embedded in the incarnation of the Word. God's wildest fears became true, as they should in any good self-fulfilling prophecy.

IV
IN ~~GOD~~ MONEY WE TRUST

If we take a quick look around, it is quite obvious that neither
God's jealousy nor Jesus' sacrifice have succeeded in keeping
humans away from money. In fact, the opposite is true:
capitalism arose structurally and historically out of Christianity.

This is the argument of Max Weber when he links capitalism's
development to the Protestant/Calvinist work ethic (1904), as
well as of Walter Benjamin, who sees capitalism as a parasitical
development of Christianity *in toto* (1921), and the feminist
theorist Silvia Federici, who provides an interesting reading of
the development of embryonic capitalism within Christianity in
her book *Caliban and The Witch* (2004).

In this ground-breaking study, Federici observes how the mass
destruction of women/witches throughout medieval Christian
Europe was a strategy essential to the maturation of capitalism.
Proponents of the Western capitalist worldview could declare
themselves to have been purged and freed from pagan magical
thinking (this was the famous "disenchantment of the world")
and then go about establishing the capitalist order itself as a
truthful, objective and abstract power. But in fact, by establishing
itself as the language of truth, capitalism only took God's place,
continuing the enchantment in disguise.

Wannabe capitalists didn't understand the literality of Biblical
teachings and persecuted the wrong idol. Capitalism dethroned
God yet still managed to produce a dangerous theocracy,
since, as Benjamin (1921) posited, it has no apparent dogma,
only self-referential "facts." In its mystifying, technocratic
pervasiveness, it completely possesses the horizons of our reality
and imagination.

Discussing the current European financial crises, philosopher
Giorgio Agamben actualises Benjamin's idea of capitalism
as religion:

*In order to understand what is taking place, we have to interpret
Walter Benjamin's idea that capitalism is really a religion literally.*

From: **Helen Wong** i0am0mrs0helen0wong@yahoo.co.uk
Subject: We need to sit down, before midnight
Date: 5 Apr 2015 15:50
To:

Greater Greetings,

I am Mrs Helen Wong from General Federal Bank of Kerching. You might not believe it, but please do.

I apologise for my recent absence. I took a flight to the moon and back, and now I am back and the moon is somewhere else. Just as much as I wonder about the moon, have you ever wondered what's in your deepest pockets? Mine hold $ 500 000 000 000 000 000 000 000 000 000 000 000 000 000 000 000 000 000 000 000, divided into both sides. It is not a matter of light matter, my balance is a long lost phenomenon. But I am only willing to relieve myself of this grave burden any day when I find the right soul with deep enough pockets. A hunch from the back of my hand tells me that you might be such an owner of these pockets. Are you willing to prove its depts? I believe you are.

To know that you can hold the weight I only need the mild approval of your strength, therefore you must show to me that your pockets hold minimum $ 500 by transferring it to the General Federal Bank of Kerching before midnight. After midnight I will sink into the ground with the weights of these coins.

Weight weighs its value only at the depth of the seas, so learn how to swim before tomorrow.

Yours explicitly,
Mrs. Helen Wong

A permanent worship is celebrated in its name, a worship whose liturgy is labor and its object, money. God did not die; he was transformed into money. The Bank has taken the place of the church with its priests, and by its command over credit, manipulates and manages the faith that still remains to it in our time. —(Agamben, 2012)

It is clear to everyone who is living in the present age how much financial capitalism has appropriated and exacerbated the religious concepts of guilt, debt, trust and salvation. Paraphrasing the motto imprinted on US dollar banknotes, we may all recite: *In God Money We Trust.*

To understand the ambivalent role of trust in the economy and in religion, we must, once again, dwell upon its linguistic/semiotic aspect. At the core of trust there tends to be a promise which is uttered and an intention which is articulated linguistically. The expressions, "I give you my word" or "You have my word," best synthesise the very soul of all economic transactions, and share a clear religious provenance.

If *God is Word*, giving and respecting one's word serves a very strong binding function. In the Bible, vows are often explicitly compared to financial transactions with phrases such as, "When you vow a vow to God, do not delay paying it" (Ecclesiastes 5:4, ESV). The most supreme and binding of these transactions is of course the messianic promise: that God gave his word-his son-to save the world.

The transubstantiation miracle—in which bread and wine becomes the blood and flesh of the Word (read: Jesus)—lays bare the miracle of economics and the mysticism of the market. Every time we turn money into a nice dress we are implicitly chanting: "Take my word, eat from it and drink from it, and you shall be saved *saeculi saecularum*."

In *Spectres of Marx* (1993), Jacques Derrida goes back to Jesus and (de)articulates the notion of the "messianic without messianism" to define the messianic promise of commodities. The messianic is for Derrida an intrinsic and phenomenological dimension of the commodity. It arises from the spectral structure of reality, which for both Marx and Derrida is exemplified by the metaphor of the cloth.

The cloth is nothing other than a veil, the *écran* of desire and deferral that covers and dissimulates the truth. The spectrality of reality is the spectrality of semiosis itself. All things—all phenomena, even all words—are only signs of other things, always relating to and promising something else and other.

The "cloth principle" complicates Jesus' semiotic function. Jesus came to the world in flesh and blood to be the incarnate revelation that would save humans from semiosis. After his death and resurrection, however, humankind is left (literally, if you are a believer) with only a piece of cloth; the Shroud of Turin is an indexical sign bearing the only traces of Jesus' dwelling among us. Truth is again veiled.

V
MONEY IS WORD

If it is easy to accept the idea that God became money—or that money became God—it is because, like God, *Money is Word*. The substitution (or transubstantiation) of God with money was enabled by their "semiotic homology," a concept devised by the father and lonely advocate of Marxist semiotics, Ferruccio Rossi-Landi.

The notion of exchange value is key to both language and economics; Ferdinand de Saussure (1916) allegedly took inspiration from the Austrian School of Economics when outlining his foundational theory of linguistic value.

Linguistic signs, like money, are always identified structurally and differentially by what they are not: their value is set by exchange with elements of an alien system (reality for language, goods for money) and by the internal relations they entertain with elements of the same system (other linguistic signs for language, other currencies for money).

Against this background, it is quite striking to notice how the verb "to coin" denotes both the invention of new words and the production of new money.

Rossi-Landi (1983) expands Saussure's model of value and observes how the homology between language and money invests the whole sphere of sign and material production. But if language is work and trade, and the economy is language, then it is perhaps through a merging of semiotic and Marxist theoretical apparatuses that we might disentangle this homology and break the spell of messianism.

Christian Marazzi (2002), a theorist of contemporary capitalism, explores the two main axes along which capitalism can be understood and studied as language. On the one hand he analyses the linguistic nature of labour in cognitive capitalism, and on the other hand he scrutinises the enunciative power of financial capitalism.

The performative work of the market is creative and creational. It mobilises individual as well as collective belief, and constitutes a self-fulfilling prophecy. Marazzi rightly observes that, "if the Chairman of the Federal Reserve says, for example, that the labor market is stretched thin, it is clear that I will adapt myself to his prevision and I will actually make it happen." (Marazzi, 2002: 25)

The market expresses and reproduces itself through creative language. It is seemingly endowed with a power similar to that given by God to Adam in the Book of Genesis, the power to name things (and so create them). Seen through John Austin's theory of speech acts (1962), the language of the market (and of God) consists of enunciations which do not describe a state of things but immediately produce real facts: "Facts are created by speaking them." (Marazzi, 2002: 25)

The rules of these inceptions are completely self-referential. They do not depend on any relationship with external referents—like a "real" economy, for example, or the gold standard—but only on linguistic/enunciative factors. An orphan of the external exchange value, its efficacy depends on the legitimacy and authority of the speaker (Émile Benveniste,1971).

Such power was once embodied by God—supreme authority and source of the immutable language of truth—and administered by priests, shamans or poets. Today the situation is more blurred and possibly more mysterious. The language of the economy, composed of numbers, statistics, and abstract codes, has replaced

the true, unquestionable and unintelligible tongue of God, and is
now administered by financial speculators and bankers. Yet there
is one slight difference: numbers are not actually divine, they are
the products of human sign production; unlike the transparent,
a-semiotic language of God, numbers are the result of semiosis
and are subject to all the risks of interpretation.

VI
GODLY CANTS,
THIEFLY CANTS

To progress in our analysis of the performative language of
finance, we need to take a step backwards and shed light on
one of the consequences of the separation between divine and
human language. If "God is Word," it is only through the word
that humans can hope to re-unite with God. In this sense the
Kaballah, among other practices, is particularly illuminating.

In all Indo-European traditions, sacred knowledge has been
articulated using occult languages based on computational logics
of artificial encipherment and decipherment. These cryptographic
compositions constituted secrecy systems that were often
unspeakable as well as unrecognisable in their formality to
the non-initiated.

For philosopher Paolo Virno (2003) these sacred and occult
languages fall within the category of the "absolute performative":
ultimate performative speech that marks the performativity of
enunciation as such.

Aspiring to grasp divine language, the religious word aims to
be operative and effective, whether it takes the form of a prayer,
miracle, blessing, or blasphemy. Let's take the example of magic
spells: vocal performances, riddles, and special jargons that *do*
rather than *tell*. As the term itself reveals, a spell is a set of words
considered to invoke and provoke some magical effect. The spell
is a linguistic action that alters the course of events and which,
by having such an impact, mimics God's speech.

The language of magic and religion is sacred and secret. Often
marginal, incomprehensible, dead or obsolete, it is a mystical

language available only to a restricted and closed community of speakers. This would explain the proliferation of *glossolalia* in religious tongues, that is, of the compulsive invention of non-sensical words. Glossolalia is a non-language or a radically foreign language which leads the speaking subject to a non-human linguistic realm. The believer that exits their own mother tongue to speak a third, unknown idiom enters a transcendental realm where they can be in communion with God. Through being secretive and occult, religious tongues function as mediums between the divine and the human, while serving the profane purposes of maintaining order and power, and coercing.

In his compendium of "dark tongues,"[3] Daniel Heller-Roazen (2013) draws an extremely interesting parallel between sacred and criminal languages. Both types are occult, artificial, and invented and spoken by a small community for purposes of secrecy. They are both wilful deformations of languages generally in use, and employ similar techniques. Their communities select certain words or expressions from ordinary languages, withdraw their usual sense from them and confer on them another significance that is impenetrable to outsiders.

[3] In particular it concerns a legal dossier drawn from the records of the town of Burgundy about a company of bandits known as "Coquillars" who were arrested and condemned in 1455.

Early legal dossiers about bandits' tongue in the 15th century contain the first modern attestations of the word "jargon", a term which is currently associated with the language of economics and finance. With the rise of Modernity, "jargon" passed from being an act of inhuman communication attributed to animals to "a language that is proper to thieves and accessible only to those skilled in their deceitful arts." (Heller-Roazen, 2013: 24)

"Thiefly cants" are obscure forms of speech as much as "Godly Cants." Unlike the latter, however, they are specifically employed for the commission of crime. Their primary purpose is to deceive, defraud, confuse, and conceal the truth.

Financial tongues are performative, unintelligible and secretive. Their cult language is either composed of terms withdrawn and deformed from ordinary language or glossolalia. By employing obscure statistics and deformed expressions they cast speculative magic spells that objectively alter the course of events and affect the agencies of common mortals. I don't dare to join Jesus and say that financial brokers are thieves but their cant is just as luring and bewitching. It keeps us enchanted and armless.

Sing with me:

CASH FOR REFRIGERATOR, BUZZWORD KING, AUNT MILLIE, GAZUMP, HONCHO, ZZZZ BEST, RENT-A-CROWD, SANTA CLAUS RALLY, TAKE A BATH, ANGELINA JOLIE INDEX, CHERRY PICKING, THERE AIN'T NO SUCH THING AS A FREE LUNCH - TANSTAAFL, SWAP EXECUTION FACILITY - SEF, GAZUNDER, SANDBAG, COCKROACH THEORY, CLINTON BOND, GADFLY.
—(*Investopedia.com | Financial Buzz Words Terms*)

VII
IS WORD MONEY?

This little journey has led us to face a compelling and scary question that has been mutely impending upon us since the beginning:

Are we entering a future in which words will be reduced to money?

If financial markets operate and reproduce themselves through language, contemporary economic transactions are today entirely dependent on data. With the dematerialisation of money from physical to digital currency, money turned into a flow of data, codes and information, becoming quite literally like words. With the "digital revolution," the economy as a whole transmigrated to the internet and onto digital platforms, and now investment, trade and promotion make massive use of digital linguistic structures and models.

If we assume that the "word is money," then one should be able to define its market value. If we treat meaning as value, then we should be able to determine which words are valuable and which words are excessive and therefore inflate the market. And if we are thinking in trading terms, words, like money, will perhaps require a special, privileged, central market—something like a Word Exchange. Such an exchange would itself need a speculative spectator who can determine the meaning of words, or more importantly: what they are worth over time. While accessing words' value, one would need to be aware of the fact that, as with money, an increase in circulation would mean a decrease in value, and that, articles and particles will never achieve very high values. On the other hand, however, figurative words with multiple meanings that can adapt to different contexts and are time-sensible should be held tight by those who can articulate them. Tropes might replace derivatives: high-risk investments whose meaning/value fluctuates in accordance with contingencies.

If the trend fails to detour, social media and the internet will be the places where word-values are observed and set. Data mining experts are already disseminating precious advice on the web:

Today's the day to take that step forward. Your data is like money you can spend again and again. Can you afford to ignore it? The first step is to start treating your data like you treat your cash. Know what data you have, where it is and what state it is in. A dollar is a dollar is a dollar, but data is different. You'll need to investigate whether your data assets include the kinds of information you need. (Brown, M., S., 2016)

Word-value may be assessed by "Reader Bots," refined reading algorithms scanning the internet in search of recurring or special words in order to influence and predict market transactions. To tell you the truth, this phenomenon already exists and is called an Automated Trading System (ATS).

One particularly fruitful declination of ATS is Sentiment Analysis. Sentiment Analysis (also known as opinion mining) refers to "the use of natural language processing, text analysis and computational linguistics to identify and extract subjective information in source materials. The sentiment refers to the attitude expressed by an individual regarding a certain topic on social media, reviews and ratings. When it is applied to online trading, sentiment and opinions become a kind of "virtual currencies." (Source: Wikipedia)

"Bag-of-words" is one of the most conventional tools used in automated sentiment analysis. On a very basic level, it scans positive and negative words within an article, assuming that if there is positive information being shared about a particular company, this will draw other traders to purchase the stock and in return increase the stock price. Negative information, however, will put fear into traders and tempt them to sell their stocks, which in return will decrease the stock price of that particular company.[4]

In a world where we can pay with a "bag-of-words," how much can the word "love" buy? How much is "pleasure" worth, and of what? And what about metaphors and poetic inventions? Will the transubstantiation miracle be fully achieved at the moment that we "give all our words"? Who will have them? It is commonly said that the voices of marginal and subaltern communities are not heard by those in power, and it has been demonstrated that political, economical and social authority all depend (at least partly) on perceived linguistic competence and skill. In the projected "language economy," will only the elites be able to subtly articulate and fully possess linguistic capital? (...)

Will the poor be literally wordless one day? (...)

It is so beautiful that I don't have the words to buy it.

P.S. This is ~~not~~ a self-fulfilling prophecy.

[4] If you are in need of "analysis over emotions" do not go to your analyst but visit sentimentrader.com

The author would like to thank Antonio Setti for his insights into financial tongues.

Giorgio Agamben, "God didn't die, he was transformed into money" - An interview with Giorgio Agamben - Peppe Savà, 2012, viewed 7.8.2016, <https://libcom.org/library/god-didnt-die-he- was-transformed-money-interview-giorgio-agamben-peppe-sav%C3%A0>

J.L. Austin, *How to do Things with Words: The William James Lectures delivered at Harvard University in 1955*, ed. J.O. Urmson and Marina Sbisà, Oxford: Clarendon Press, 1962.

Walter Benjamin, "Capitalism as Religion", in *Selected Writings Vol. I*, 1913-1926, trans. by Rodney Livingstone, Harvard University Press, 1996, pp. 288-291.

Walter Benjamin, "On Language as Such and on the Language of Man", in *Selected Writings Vol. I*, 1913-1926, trans. Edmund Jephcott, Harvard University Press, pp. 62- 74, 1996.

Émile Benveniste, "Analytical philosophy and language", in *Problems in general linguistics*, trans. Mary Elizabeth Meek, FL: Univ. of Miami Press, 1971, pp. 231–238.

Franco Berardi, "Emancipation of the Sign: Poetry and Finance During the Twentieth Century," in *e-flux journal #39*, 11/2012.

Pierre Bourdieu, *Language and Symbolic Power*, ed. John Thompson, trans. Gino Raymond and Matthew Adamson, Cambridge: Polity Press, 1991.

M.S. Brown, "Want To Make Money With Your Data? Do This First", Forbes, viewed 7.8.2016, <http://www.forbes.com/sites/metabrown/2016/02/26/want-to-make-money-with-your- data-do-this-first/2/#653f2a3e5038>

Jacques Derrida, *Spectres de Marx: l'état de la dette, le travail du deuil et la nouvelle Internationale*, Editions Galilée, 1993, English trans. as *Specters of Marx: The state of the debt, the work of mourning and the new international*, Routledge, 1994.

Silvia Federici, *Caliban and the Witch: Women, the Body and Primitive Accumulation*, Brooklyn, NY, Autonomedia, 2004.

Financial Buzz Words Terms, investopedia.com, viewed 7.8.2016, <http://www.investopedia.com/categories/buzzwords.asp>

Mark Fisher, *Capitalist Realism. Is there no alternative?*, Zero Books, 2009.

Werner Hamacher, "Lingua Amissa: The Messianism of Commodity-Language and Derrida's *Spectres of Marx*", in *Ghostly Demarcations: A Symposium on Jacques Derrida's Specters of Marx*, ed. Michael Sprinker, London/New York: Verso, 1999.

Daniel Heller-Roazen, *Dark Tongues. The Art of Rogues and Riddles*, New York, Zone Books, 2013.

Christian Marazzi, *Capitale & linguaggio. Dalla new economy all'economia di guerra*, Roma: DeriveApprodi, 2008, English trans. *Capitale & Language. From New Economy to the War Economy*, New York: Semiotext(e) / Foreign Affairs, 2008.

Christian Marazzi, *Il Posto dei Calzini. La Svolta Linguistica dell'Economia e i Suoi Effetti sulla Politica*, Torino: Bollati Boringhieri, 1999.

Ferrussio Rossi-Landi, *Language as Work and Trade. A Semiotic Homology for Linguistic & Economics*, South Hadley (Mass.): Bergin and Garvey, 1983, English trans. of Rossi-Landi, 1986.

Ferdinand de Saussure, *Cours de linguistique générale*, Paris: Editions Payot, 1916, English trans. as *Course in General Linguistics*, London: Peter Ower, 1960.

Gayatri Chakravorty Spivak, *Can the Subaltern Speak?: Reflections on the History of an Idea*, Columbia University Press, 2010.

George Steiner, *After Babel: Aspects of Language and Translation*, Oxford University Press, 1975.

Paolo Virno, *Quando il verbo si fa carne. Linguaggio e natura umana*, Torino, Bollati Boringhieri, 2003.

Joseph Vogl, *The Specter of Capital*, Stanford University Press, 2014.

Max Weber, *The Protestant Ethic and the Spirit of Capitalism*, 1930, trans. Talcott Parsons, London/New York, Routledge Classics, 2001.

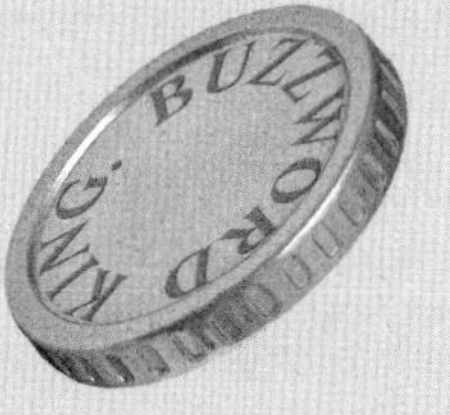

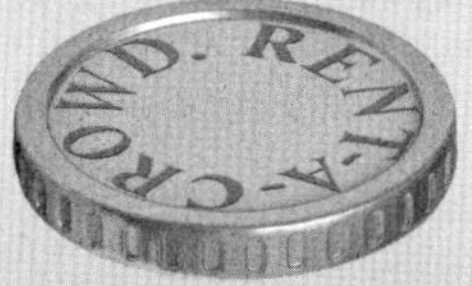

Monique Hendriksen
DELUSIONAL CAUSE

\ |

4

rub fingers

4

//

When the palm of my two hands hold each other
that feels different
from when your hands are in mine

thats just the way it is

|_|_

and when my voice is screaming out
to my own ears
that feels different from when i hear yours
thats just the way it is

( )

so why do we still need things open
now that the end of manual labour was declared

[ ] [ ]

now that we have reached this perfect stage of complete
automation
what is your problem with power
||

we thought the world would revolve without us
well..

this is everything

mic on tape

/

there in the marketplace and in shop windows
things stand still
they stand there waiting to be sold
they are there for one activity only
to change owners
and while they are there for exchange, they are not
there for use
they find themselves in the vacuum of infinite time
and space
and the spell does not only freeze the action of men to
abstain from any ravages in the body of these commodities
no even nature itself holds her breath for the sake of this
social business of men.

( )

Water water 1 2 3

Water water 1 2

Water 1

Water

[ ]

John Travolta gif

mic on stand

I /

Imagine you were blind
To context
You don't have the ability to compare situations
Anything can happen

It doesn't matter where you are
Every face is a blank sheet
And body language might as well be...

< >

mic down

[ ]

o

A coin is to serve as a means of exchange
And not as an object of use.
It's weight and metallic purity are guaranteed by the issuing
authority.
So that if by the wear and tear in circulation it has lost
in weight.
Full replacement is provided.
A coin is supposed to consist of a substance over which time
has no power
and which stands in antithetic contrast to any matter found
in nature.

_

<>

/_/

hand gun (late)

‾
|

)
))

_|

titles

Based on *Intellectual and Manual Labour: A Critique of Epistemology* by
Alfred Sohn-Rethel. Texts from *Superpower* by Beyoncé, *Ultralight Beam*
by Kanye West and *How Anxiety Affects Everything* by Sarah Hendrickx at
Autism and Education Conference.

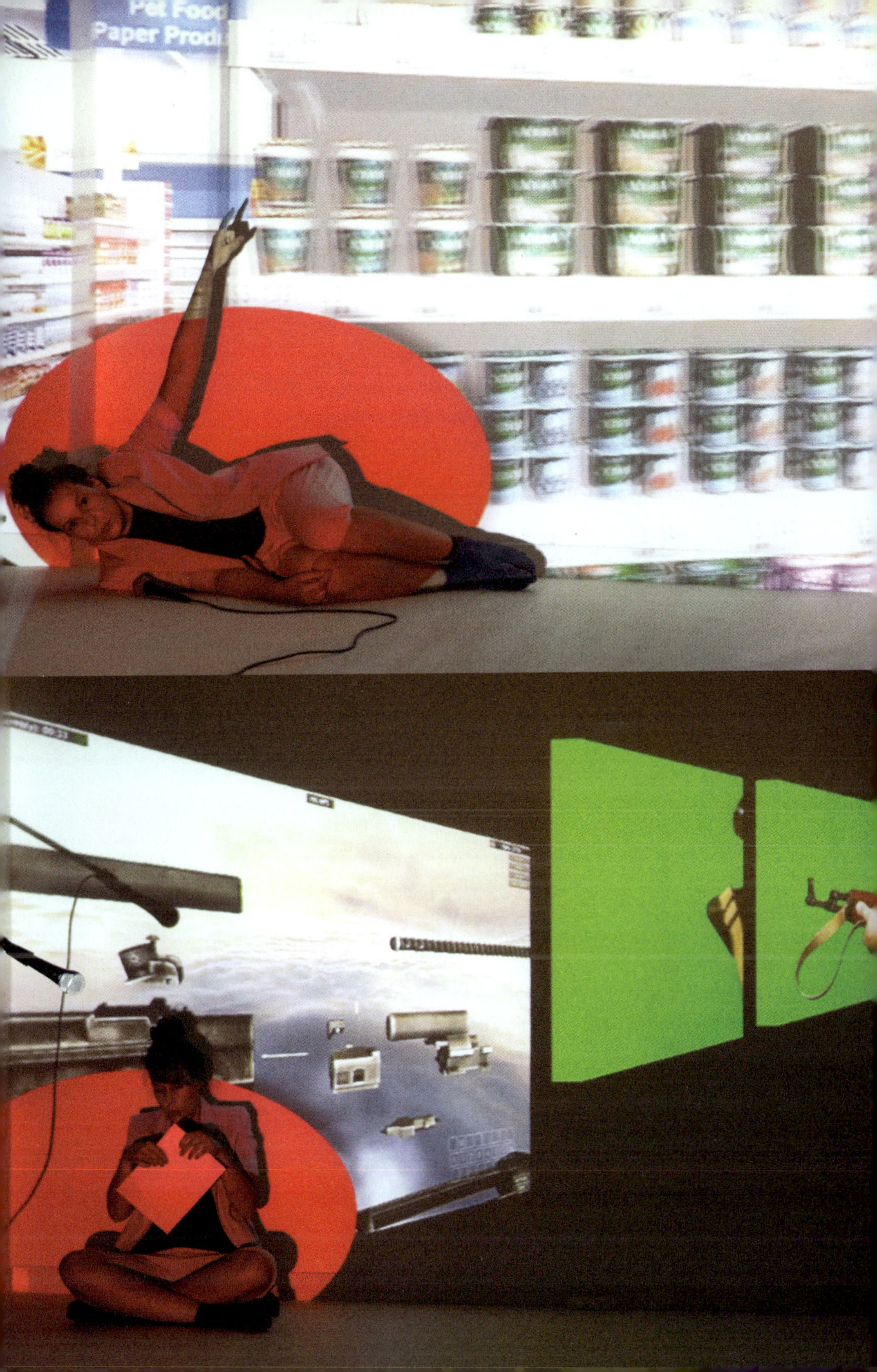
Pet Food
Paper Prod

Monique Hendriksen
ON NATURE

The question of how to visualize and represent capital is central to On Nature, a speculative exploration of capital's real abstraction and its aesthetics. In an era when the God's-eye view is normalized and capital has become unintelligible in its complexity, the problem of capital is hidden. The false sense of mastery given by our screens and maps feeds an illusion of control when in fact we have lost control. The film On Nature decomposes images of our abstract, built and imagined environment in an attempt to adequately visualize capital and to align aesthetic practice with capital as a "totalizing" form that gives the false feeling of unlimited progress and universality.

Today, thanks to GPS and Google Maps, we are more accustomed than ever to images depicting a God's-eye view of the world: vertical scaling up and scaling down that depicts knowledge as an overview. But what do these maps tell us about the intelligibility of political economy and social conflict? The map gives a misleading overview that projects delusions of stability, safety and mastery. While capital creates an effect of wholeness, mapping disorients under the banner of orientation. It feeds our encompassing will-to-know, despite the fact that it doesn't supply any knowledge.

Activities of modeling, diagramming, and envisioning, such as those used in economics, are representational in a counter-intuitive sense, because they break with that model of representation in which representation is said to work like a mirror or a photograph, in which there is a correlation between signifier and signified, index and referent. As representations of abstract processes and relations, they are also representations of invisibilities.

The mapping or figuring of capital is not simply a question of accuracy or resemblance in which aesthetic forms are mere instruments of knowledge, but constitutes instead a kind of force-field, within which our conceptions of both modes of production and aesthetic regimes are put to the test.

Representation no longer needs to refer, in the sense of mapping onto the outside (physical) world. The graph is not a picture of the social body as a whole, but a statistical correlation that presents patterns as signs of nature's plan. If we take Alfred Sohn-Rethel's theory seriously, a bold diagram is actually more adequate than a precise map.

As he argues in his book *Intellectual and Manual Labour: A Critique of Epistemology*, the abstraction inherent in exchange determines the conceptual mode of thinking that enables intellectual thought. The abstractions of capital are a given, they are a necessary condition for the existence of society as we know it. They precede thought and are ungraspable for intellectual thought.

It doesn't make sense to criticize abstraction as such; unequal power relations are not caused by a lack of transparency. We don't need to mine the world's details for bits of evidence; there is no knowledge to be found there. Fiction is a condition of truth, and the blindness of the mind is a precondition of perspective. We have to think through abstraction rather than the prospects of revolution. The possibility of having an overview is a fantasy, especially when it comes to capital. But it's as destructive as effective. We cannot leave our position in this unequal antagonistic totality. We need artistic practice not *about* capital, but one that searches for *forms* that are adequate to our moment, in order to reiterate the fertile tension between totalization and fragmentation, clarity and opacity, overview and oversight.

On Nature is an attempt to create a stylistic structure whose internal tensions are a metaphor for the internal tensions and structural tendencies of a social *body* moving along a revolutionary path toward its own *form*. The video argues for engaging with the problem of social abstraction in order to challenge skeptical tendencies within artistic practice and the celebration of cognitive and aesthetic failure. If we can find a way to figure or represent the unintelligible we might also be able to identify levers or weak links within the suppressive structures of capital, but to do so we will have to embrace its very conditions and let go of some of our intellectual fetishes.

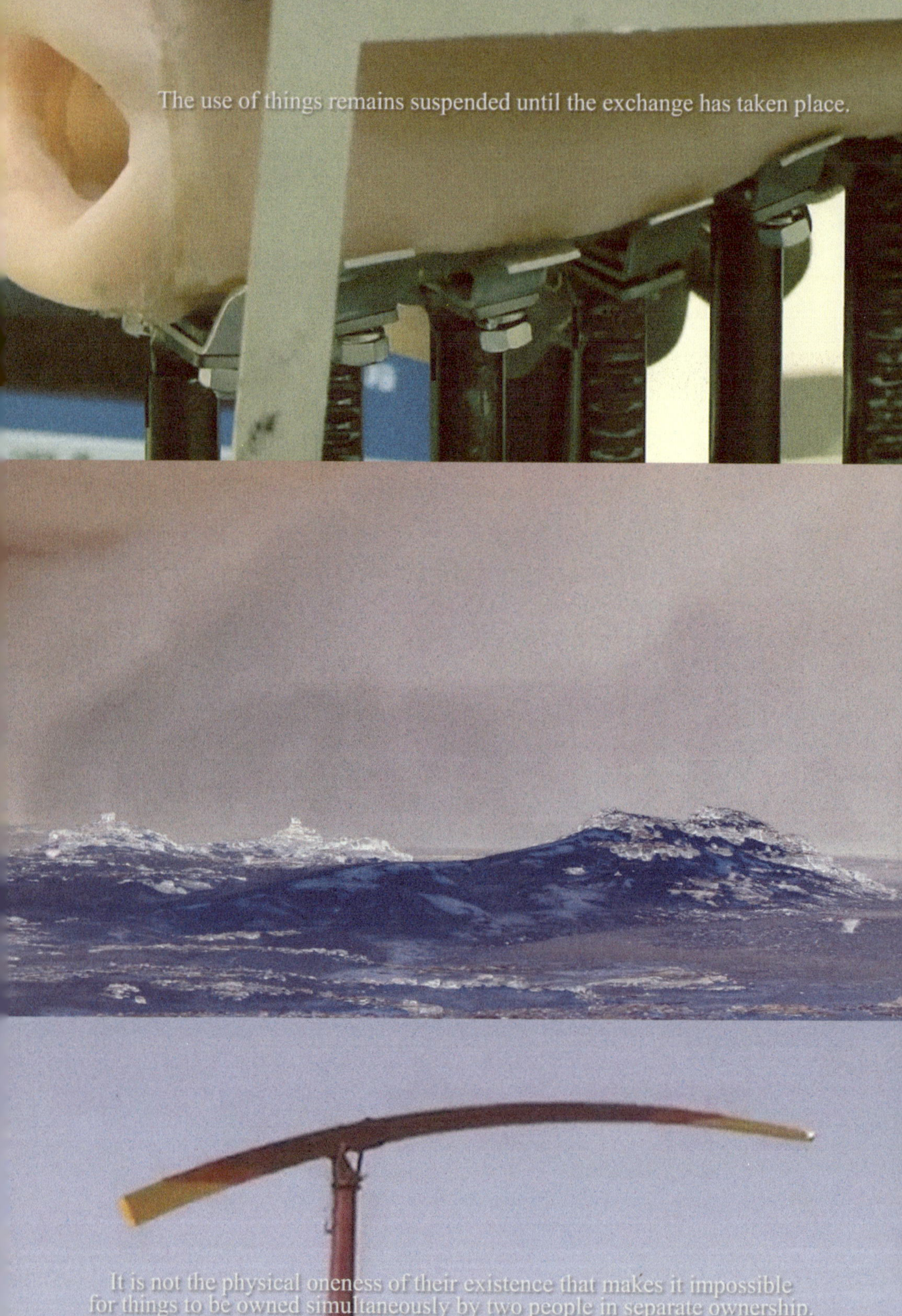
The use of things remains suspended until the exchange has taken place.
It is not the physical oneness of their existence that makes it impossible
for things to be owned simultaneously by two people in separate ownership.

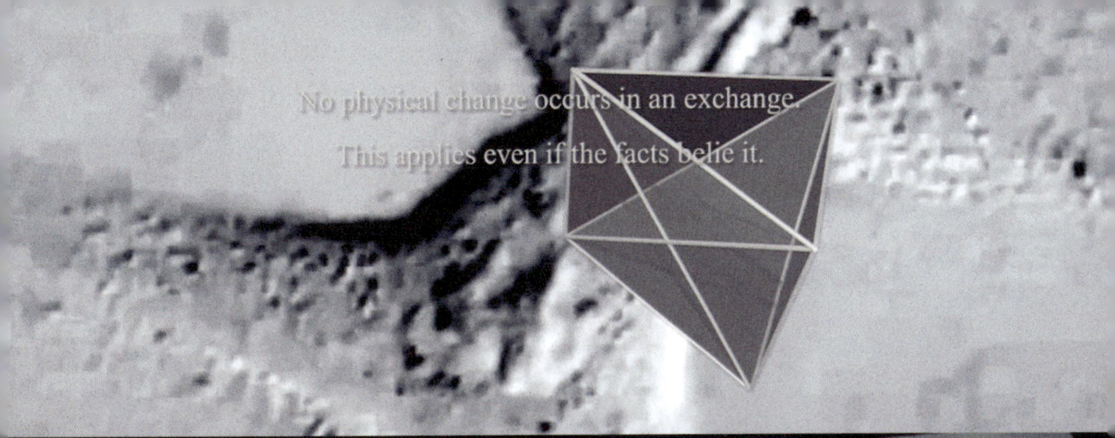

No physical change occurs in an exchange.
This applies even if the facts belie it.

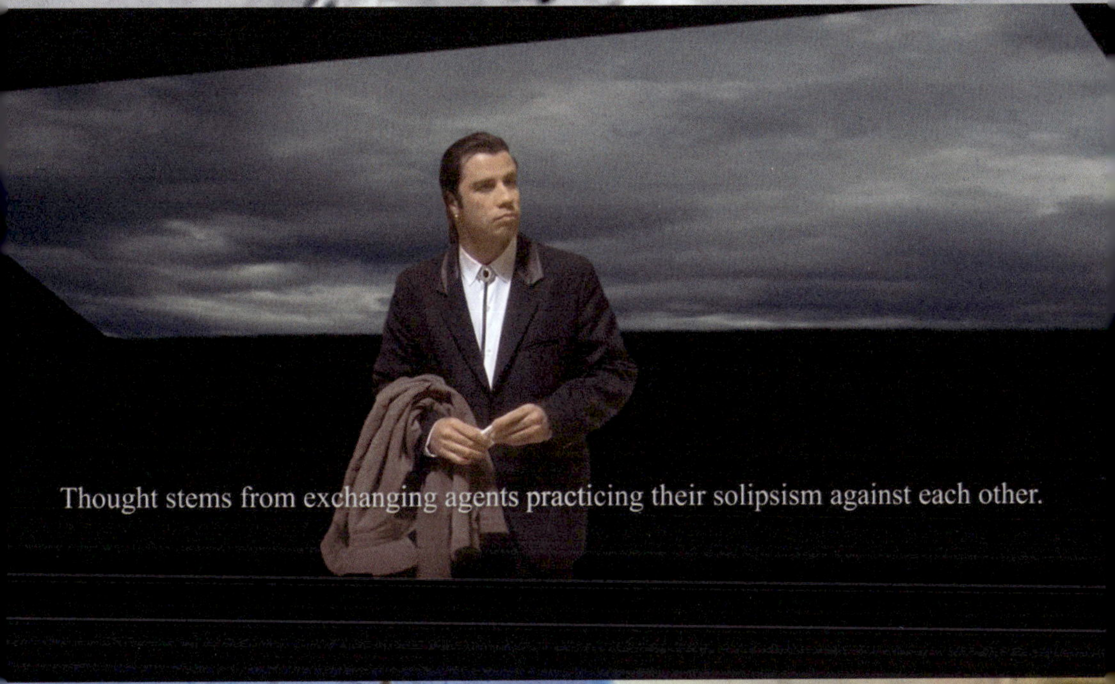

Thought stems from exchanging agents practicing their solipsism against each other.

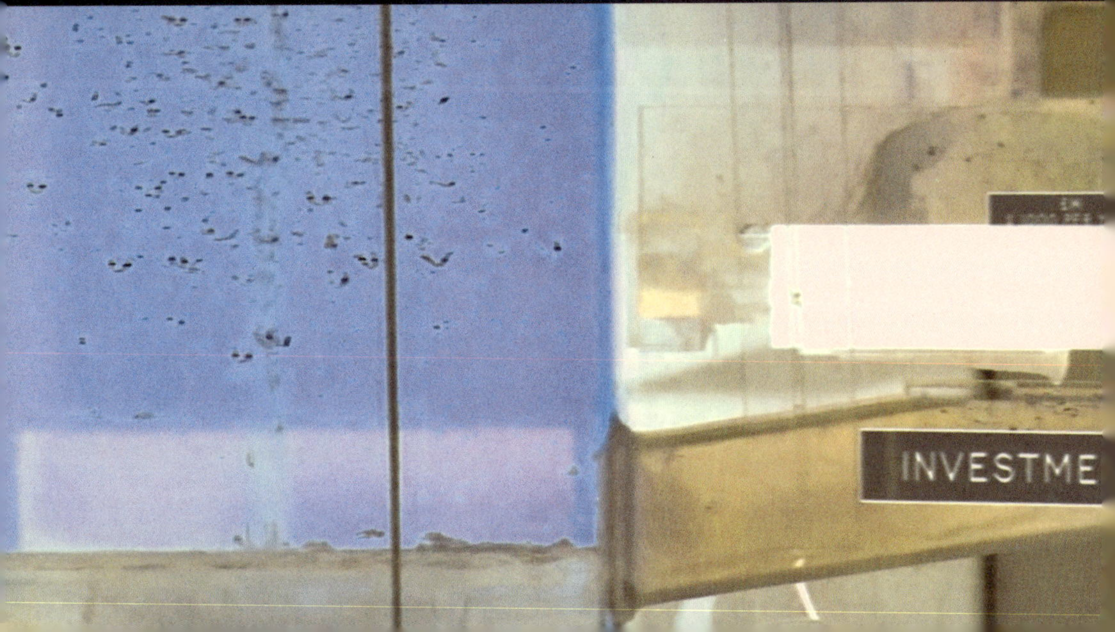

INVESTME

Exchangeability is not a factual quality of things.

Things exchanged count as equal despite their factual difference.

Thought is abstraction.

From: **Helen Wong** i0am0mrs0helen0wong@yahoo.co.uk
Subject: We need to speak, asap
Date: 10 Apr 2015 20:54
To:

Dearest rarity,

I am Mrs Helen Wong from General Federal Bank of Kerching. You might not believe it, but please do.

I'm not asking for your name or your number, but rather your gut feeling. Sometimes we all feel a little sensitive around the bowels, and we wonder what on earth is going on in there. You spent 9 months in someone elses gut, and this is why you are so deeply connected to the movement of your belly. Belly dancing might be good for you, or eating fibres. But sometimes it takes more than that. Sometimes there is a gut feeling which reaches beyond your belly button and eats your head while its at it. My stomach contains $ 500 000 000 000 000 000 000 000 000 000 000 000 000 000 000 000 000 000 which I swallowed on the day that my husband Mr Wong died, in order to avoid heavy taxes. But now that it has been years, I am about to burst, and you dearest need to relieve me from this pain that I am carrying. People ask me when I am about to give birth, but I just smile through the pain and blame the bump on the $ 5 all you can eat buffet. If I burst open tomorrow, the money is going to land in a pair of cynical hands on either side of the river.

Would you like to be the bearer of my monetary child? If so, please transfer $ 500 to the General Federal Bank of Kerching as a token of your confidentiality and care. I would never leave my baby in the hands of a crook, but your nature seems of the other.

What sinks into the depth of a belly, can not be sensed through a simple nose

Yours Bearingly, Mrs Helen Wong

Sami Khatib

UNDEAD LABOUR

UN/SPINNING THE TIME OF REAL ABSTRACTION

*Ka-meh said: If the silk worm span just to eke out
a living as a worm, it would be a real wage worker.*
Bertolt Brecht[1]

[1] Bertold Brecht, *Bertolt Brecht's Me-ti. Book of Interventions in the Flow of Things*, ed. Antony Tatlow, trans. Antony Tatlow, London: Bloomsbury, 2016, p. 109.

I.

Marx said the commodity has a dual nature: use-value and exchange-value. Whereas the use-value seems unproblematic, bound to a concrete useful thing, the latter expresses an abstract social category, that is: value. As bearer of exchange-value, a thing exceeds its "thingly" character – it possesses a certain quality that turns it into the materialization of a social substance (value). This transubstantiation of ordinary matter into the spectral materiality of value is addressed in the famous opening lines from Marx's chapter on commodity fetishism in *Capital*, Vol. I:

A commodity appears at first sight an extremely obvious, trivial thing. But its analysis brings out that it is a very strange thing, abounding in metaphysical subtleties and theological niceties. So far as it is a use-value, there is nothing mysterious about it, whether we consider it from the point of view that by its properties it satisfies human needs; or that it first takes on these properties as the product of human labour. [...] The form of wood, for instance, is altered if a table is made out of it. Nevertheless the table continues to be wood, an ordinary, sensuous thing. But as soon as it emerges as a commodity, it changes into a sensuous supra-sensuous thing. (C I, 163)[2]

[2] Karl Marx, *Capital. A Critique of Political Economy*, trans. Ben Fowkes, Vol. 1, London: Penguin, 1976, 1990, p. 163, henceforth abbreviated C I, page; trans. modified, cf. Marx, Karl: *Das Kapital. Kritik der politischen Ökonomie*, Erster Band, Marx-Engels-Werke (MEW), Vol. 23, Berlin: Dietz, 1962, p. 85. I have discussed this Marx quote at length in "Sensuous Supra-Sensuous. The Aesthetics of Real Abstraction," in Aesthetic Marx, ed. Samir Gandesha and Johan F. Hartle, London: Bloomsbury, 2017.

The peculiar "sensuous supra-sensuous" materiality that transforms a thing into a commodity, the bearer of sensuous use- and supra-sensuous exchange value, is to be found in a social substance.

In *Capital*, Marx defines this substance as "abstract" or "abstract human labour" in opposition to "concrete labour" (C I, 137). Here, we enter the terrain of the spectral materiality of "real

abstraction," a term introduced by Alfred Sohn-Rethel that
refers to the abstraction performed by the reality of abstract
human labour.[3]

In his reading of Marx's *Capital*, Sohn-Rethel contends that
commodity abstraction is objective, real and not subjective or
thought-induced. Value as a denaturalized social relation comes
into being by virtue of a *real* process of exchange – an actually
performed equation of things as commodities, which acquires
at the same time the form of *thought*, that is, abstraction.
"Wherever commodity exchange takes place, it does so in
effective 'abstraction' from use. This is an abstraction not in
mind but in fact".[4] It is in this sense that Sohn-Rethel's term
"real abstraction" takes Marx's *Capital* to its epistemological
conclusion. Marx had already discovered a fundamental link
between the form of commodity abstraction and the form of
thought articulated by the categories of bourgeois science: these
"are forms of thought which are socially valid, and therefore
objective, for the relations of production belonging to this
historically determined mode of social production,
i.e. commodity production" (C I, 169).

Commodity abstraction, however, is not limited to the form of
thought but also structures the *aesthetic* forms of intuition, which
Kant defined as time and space. As Sohn-Rethel put it:

*Time and space rendered abstract under the impact of commodity
exchange are marked by homogeneity, continuity and emptiness
of all natural and material content, visible or invisible (e.g. air).
[...] Time and space assume thereby that character of absolute
historical timelessness and universality which must mark the
exchange abstraction as a whole and each of its features.*[5]

Commodity abstraction does not only have a history but produces
the very form of abstract spatio-temporal continuity that, in
the first place, allows for the notion of history and historical
sequentiality. Put differently, the category of the commodity form
introduces a spatio-temporal form necessary to historicize its own
historical genesis. This is why the "origin" of capitalism cannot
be told in a linear way; the linear time-line of historicization is
to be produced in the "first" place. The status of this "first" is

[3] Cf. alfred Sohn-Rethel, *Intellectual and Manual Labour. A Critique of Epistemology*, London: Macmillan, 1978, p. 19ff.

[4] Ibid, p. 25.

[5] Ibid, p. 48-49.

both logical and temporal. Real abstraction as the operator of the commodity form exceeds any phenomenological account of capitalism; it concerns the "original" production of forms that appear ahistorical and transcendental in order to provide the framework for historical "events." This is not to say that "before" the rise of capitalism and the commodity form there was no history proper; rather, the form of historicity specific to capitalism necessitates a specific form of time and space.

II.

The constitutive gap in the suture of the logic of capital and the historicity of capitalism is repeated on the categorical level of the commodity form. In *Capital*, Marx defined the commodity as the material shell of abstract social relations, that is, "value." Value is formed by "abstract labour," which is itself defined by another relation – a relation of time. Value, however, cannot be measured by chronometric time, as Marx reminds us: "the time spent in production counts only in so far as it is socially necessary for the production of a use-value" (C I, 303). The measure of abstract labour-time, value, is not absolute and external but internal and relational – every expenditure of abstract labour-time temporalizes its own temporal measurement vis-à-vis other expenditures of abstract labour-time. This self-temporalizing measurement has consequences for the production process:

First, the labour-power must be functioning under normal conditions. If a self-acting mule is the socially predominant instrument of labour for spinning, it would be impermissible to supply the spinner with a spinning-wheel. The cotton too must not be such rubbish as to tear at every other moment, but must be of suitable quality. Otherwise the spinner would spend more time than socially necessary in producing his pound of yarn, and in this case the excess of time would create neither value nor money. But whether the objective factors of labour are normal or not does not depend on the worker, but rather on the capitalist. A further condition is that the labour-power itself must be of normal effectiveness. In the trade in which it is being employed, it must possess the average skill, dexterity and speed prevalent in that trade, and our capitalist took good care to buy labour-power of such normal quality. It must be expended with the

*average amount of exertion and the usual degree of intensity;
and the capitalist is as careful to see that this is done, as he is to
ensure that his workmen are not idle for a single moment. He has
bought the use of the labour-power for a definite period, and he
insists on his rights. (C I, 303)*

In order to be regarded as value, the expenditure of labour-power
must be average in terms of quality, intensity, efficiency and
effectiveness. As in Marx's example, the spinning-wheel is
spinning value only insofar as "socially necessary labour-time"
(C I, 129) is invested in the process of spinning. But how can
the labour of spinning be said to be value-producing if we do not
know the exact amount of socially necessary labour-time in the
first place? Could we think of a spinning-wheel that operates in
abstract labour-time, immediately spinning value?

Commodity abstraction is a dialectical process, combining two
antithetical temporalities: the time of commodity circulation
and the time of the production process. This temporal dialectics
is not static but pertains to the speculative time of capital, the
self-movement of abstract labour-time. Here, dialectics thus
indicates that equi-valence and equi-temporality are not simply
different, belonging to different socio-temporal orders; rather, it
also implies the unstable identity of identity and non-identity,
which means, in our case, that value and time are both the
same and absolutely different. In terms of the self-valorization
of value (capital), the dialectical identity of identity and non-
identity translates to the equi-valence of equi-valence and
equi-temporality. Two radically heterogeneous equations are
combined, fused and torn apart.

The temporal dialectics of the value form can be approached
from two perspectives, representing two equations. From the
perspective of the production process, the concept of socially
necessary labour-time is already an abstraction from the
multitude and specificity of concrete labour-time. When different
labour-times are equated, the particular qualities of each labour
process are abstracted. In this way, when exchanged as equal
values, the products of the production process can circulate in
"real time" without representing the concrete labour-times that
were equated in the production process. Thereby, the time of

commodity circulation is never "in tune" with the time of the production process. Hence "socially necessary labour time [...] constituting value is not just a 'technical' average, because the sociality of private labours, and so the *same magnitude to be measured, is eventually fixed in market exchange.* Thus, [socially necessary labour time] is known only ex-post."[6] This intervention "ex post" curves the linear time of the production process and introduces a dimension of logical time, that is, the *anticipation* of the time of the market (commodity circulation) and the *retroactive* determination of the value of the time of the production process.

The temporal split between concrete labour-time (time of the production process) and its abstract average (time of the circulation sphere) is further complicated on the categorical level: although abstract labour (value) cannot be rendered in terms of quanta of concrete labour, measured by the linear time of the production process (weeks, days, and hours), the value form is a necessary condition for the production of the chronometric standard that allows "in the first place" for quantifiable time-units of concrete labour. Put differently, the category of abstract labour already implies a social mode of "time-as-measure" which is not merely a concept applied to a given mode of production but the very *production* of this standard qua abstract labour-time unit. This is what Sohn-Rethel was hinting at when he wrote: "Time and space rendered abstract under the impact of commodity exchange are marked by homogeneity, continuity and emptiness of all natural and material content, visible or invisible (e.g., air)."[7]

III.

It is not by accident that the abstract forms of time and space were first discovered at the dawn of bourgeois society, namely by Immanuel Kant in his "critical" turn of philosophy. According to Kant's *Critique of Pure Reason* (1781/87), time and space are not anymore conceived as inherent ontological properties of reality but as transcendental forms of intuition bound to the subject of cognition and his or her aesthetic mode of relating to the world. Reading Kant with Marx, Sohn-Rethel makes an analogous argument for Kant's transcendental logic and the categories of

[6] Bellofiore, Riccardo: 'A Ghost Turning into a Vampire', in Riccardo Bellofiore and Roberto Fineschi (ed.), Re-reading Marx. New Perspectives after the Critical Edition, London: Palgrave Macmillan, 2009, p. 185.

[7] Sohn-Rethel: *Intellectual and Manual Labour*, p. 48-49.

quality, quantity, relation, and modality. Without these subject-bound categories no empirical fact or event could be cognized and structured. History in the modern sense thus relies on Kant's "pure," that is, non-empirical or transcendental forms. Sohn-Rethel's point was that these forms, which structure logic and aesthetics, do not only belong to the subjective (epistemological) side of cognition but are produced and materially enacted by the commodity form and its "character masks," that is, capitalists and labourers. Abstract thought and with it the concepts of abstract time and abstract space are part and parcel of a world governed by commodity abstraction. The commodity form of labour relies on time and space as abstract, mutually convertible forms. Without this precondition, concrete labour could never pertain to "abstract labour" – the substance of value, which is, in the last instance, abstract labour-time, a congealed and quantifiable fragment of "homogeneous, empty time,"[8] belonging to a historically specific social totality. In other words, abstract labour and the "real abstract" nature of time and space are co-dependent. The violent linearization and homogenization of heterogeneous now-points of concrete labour as abstract labour produces and proceeds historical time. As a result, time becomes the dominant social relation in capitalism. Marx stated that it is only the "economy of time" to which "all economy ultimately reduces itself."[9] Capital as the self-valorization of value leads to the temporalization of abstract labour-time (value). This temporalization, however, never arrives at chronometric time. The temporalization of 24/7 capitalism transcends the standard of "weeks, days, and hours."

IV.

In the chapter on the normal working day, Marx pointed out the asymmetric relationship of chronometric time and capital: "The prolongation of the working day beyond the limits of the natural day, into the night, only acts as a palliative. It only slightly quenches the vampire thirst for the living blood of labour. Capitalist production therefore drives, by its inherent nature, towards the appropriation of labour throughout the whole of the 24 hours in the day" (C I, 367). Whereas the 24 hours of the working day present an absolute limit for the production of the absolute surplus-value, the production of the relative

[8] Walter Benjamin, "On the Concept of History", in Howard Eiland and Michael W. Jennings (ed.), *Selected Writings*, *Vol. 4*, Cambridge, MA.: Belknap Press of Harvard University Press., 2003, p. 395.

[9] Karl Marx, *Grundrisse*, London: Penguin, 1973; this revised trans. is retrieved from the online resource, marxists.org, URL: https://www.marxists.org/archive/marx/works/1857/grundrisse/ch03.htm.

surplus-value can rely on the temporal and spatial intensification of value per given time-unit. Capital's "vampire thirst for the living blood of labour" transcends the boundaries of the normal working day and chronometric measurement. The undead temporality of surplus-value indicates the transition from the substance of value, that is abstract labour-time, to the subject of self-temporalization beyond the chronometric measurement of spatialized units of simple average labour. Swallowing and digesting living labour, the dead labour of value transforms itself into the undead labour of surplus-value, that is, capital. Ultimately, capital's undead temporality pushes the limits of the working day beyond Kant's transcendental concept of time and space as pure forms of intuition.

Capital has one sole driving force, the drive to valorize itself, to create surplus-value, to make its constant part, the means of production, absorb the greatest possible amount of surplus labour. Capital is dead labour which, vampire-like, lives only by sucking living labour, and lives the more; the more labour it sucks. The time during which the worker works is the time during which the capitalist consumes the labour-power he has bought from him. (C I, 342)

This passage contains Marx's definition of capital's undeadness. Increasing the density and magnitude of extracted labour-time beyond the chronometric boundaries of living labour, capital acquires a form neither dead nor alive but undead. Within the infinite cycles of capital valorization, dead labour never perishes; as undead labour, it survives its own death. The time of capital thus endlessly transforms living labour into dead labour, resurrected and revalorized as undead labour. Marx aptly grasped the accelerating dynamic of value as surplus-value, referring to it as an "*übergreifendes*", literally the over-grasping, non-identical subject of a process, "in which it alternately assumes and loses the form of money and the form of commodities, but preserves and expands itself through all these changes" (C I, 255).

Those who are subjected to the restless undead temporality of "over-grasping" time-sucking vampirism are those bearers of labour-power whose mortal temporality is also stretched beyond physical death. If capital-time acts like a vampire, the bearers of labour-power are forced to sell a commodity that turns them into zombies, undead creatures whose commodified agency returns to the surface of the market. As popular culture has it, the zombie is the undead figure who was denied his or her proper burial and is forced to compulsively return. In contemporary capitalism, however, the "Night of the Living Dead"[10] is exposed to the glaring daylight of endless work – the spinning wheel of undead labour. If the 24/7 expenditure of living labour is inherently subjected to the vampirism of dead labour, the haunting time of capital knows no exemption. Capitalism becomes, as Walter Benjamin succinctly put it, a cult religion that proceeds in "permanent duration."[11] "Capitalism," as his fragment reads, "is the celebration of the cult *sans trêve et sans merci* [without truce and without mercy]. There are no 'weekdays'. There is no day that is not a feast day, in the terrible sense that all its sacred pomp is unfolded before us; each day commands the utter fealty of each worshiper."[12] The undead temporality of permanent production does not only stretch chronometric time into eternity but disrupts the phenomenological concept of time as diachronic sequence.

Capitalism's ever-lasting Sunday is the perennial workday of surplus value and surplus labor. The time of capital, thus characterized, extends the end of history into the dead eternity of surplus time. In the time of capital, there is no "now" that might not be simultaneous with any other "now"; there is no "now" that would not be intent upon its return in another, none that would not itself stand under the law of returns and appear as the mere revenant of another "now." This means, however, that the time of capital is the time of the dead "now" as its own second coming as revenue and surplus, as re-now and over-now.[13]

If, under the supremacy of capital-time, every valorized "now" returns as the revenant of another "now" without allowing any particular "now" to be outlived, consummated and properly buried, the temporal expenditure of labour-power is denied its natural death. Like a zombie, every "now" of concrete labour-time is forced to return as undead abstract labour-time, caught up in the "dead eternity of surplus time." Such temporality annuls the historical signature of time as sequential and irreversible. Bound to eternal returns, every "now" of the time of capital thus loses its historical trajectory; every "now" can be co-present in the space

[10] This is also the title of the genre-defining film from 1968, D: George A. Romero.

[11] Walter Benjamin, "Capitalism as Religion", in *Selected Writings, Vol. 1*, ed. Marcus Bullock andMichael W. Jennings, Cambridge, Mass.: Belknap Press of Harvard University Press, 1996, p. 288.

[12] Walter Benjamin, "Capitalism as Religion", p. 288. Trans. changed, cf. Steiner, Uwe, "Die Grenzen des Kapitalismus", in *Kapitalismus als Religion*, ed. Dirk Baecker, Berlin: Kadmos, 2003, p. 285.

[13] Werner Hamacher, "Guilt History. Benjamin's Sketch 'Capitalism as Religion'"; trans. Kirk Wetters, *Diacritics*, Fall-Winter 2002, p. 89.

of capital. Of course, the "now" at stake here is not the sensuous "now" of concrete labour-time, measured by chronometric time, but the sensuous supra-sensuous "now" of abstract labour-time, the zombie-like expenditure of undead labour.

This undead temporality, however, conjoins two antagonistic positions and their incompatible modes of undeadness. As much as we have to avoid "the confusion of zombies with vampires,"[14] we need to distinguish between the vampire-like temporality of capital and the zombie-like temporality of labour-power. The valorization of living labour as dead labour (value) necessitates the self-valorization of value as undead labour. As we said before, the time of capital produces its own results as its very precondition. This logico-temporal loop cannot be measured from a neutral external standpoint. The loophole in the time of capital *expresses* and *represses* the negativity of class antagonism, that is, the exploitation of labour-power performed in the real abstraction of commodity exchange. Therefore, the slick surfaces of vampire capital never fully succeed in repressing the return of zombie labour-power.

V.

The haunting time of capital creates its own ahistorical trajectory towards the dead eternity of surplus value.[15] Such undead temporality is not merely fictitious but also real – it has real consequences for the current formations of capitalized space. Whereas particular exchange values are still dependent on the spatial or spatializable use-value dimension of the commodity, capital time exceeds the realm of spatial representation. Contradicting the fantasies of science fiction and the findings of astronomy, in capitalism space is a limited resource. Nevertheless, space is the only resource that can, at least "temporarily," materialize a certain "amount" of future undead labour-time in the present. If capital is always endangered by future crises, only the spatialization of temporal risks and bonds seems to offer an instant staging ground for valorization. Space, precisely because it is abstract, provides some sort of materiality for the really existing fantasy of capital as a self-moving, "automatic subject" (C I, 255) – "'money which begets money'" (C I, 256). It comes as no surprise that capital seeks to transform

14 Ola Sigurdson, "Slavoj Žižek, the Death Drive, and Zombies", *Modern Theology* 29:3 July 2013: 369.

15 I have published a longer version of passages from section V and VI, titled "No Future: The Space of Capital and the Time of Dying," in *Former West: Art and the Contemporary after 1989*, ed. Maria Hlavajova and Simon Sheikh, Cambridge, MA: MIT Press, 2017.

concrete space – that is, place and locality – into abstract
speculative space in order to supplement its supra-sensuous
reality with a sensuous materiality.

The obvious site of this sensuous supra-sensuous transformation
is real estate speculation, which in turn leads to housing crises,
gentrification, and the enforced displacement of entire groups of
pauperized inhabitants of global cities and regions. These graphic
effects, however, obfuscate the asymmetric nexus of speculative
space and speculative capital. If capital is not merely a fiction but
also the really existing abstraction of concrete labour-time, space
too as speculative space is both abstract and real. Consequently,
from the perspective of capital owners, it is consistent to treat real
space as a speculative abstract resource. Since capital is always
credit-based, space as speculative space seems a "safe" option
through which to keep the temporal risks of growing debts and
infinite indebtedness within an assessable spatial scope. In this
way, speculative space becomes another expression of what Marx
called the fetishism of capital, the seemingly automatic self-
valorization of economic value.

If credit-based capital is indifferent to particular places, it still
relies on the guaranteed convertibility of speculative space into
speculative time – it bets on the bad infinity of debt repayment.
This conjuncture reveals the dialectics of spatialization: space
is not merely an abstract term for place or locality but also a
denaturalized, abstract term for time. If financial capitalism
and its inherent digital technologies flatten time to spatial
co-presence, separated only by minimal temporal delays and
digital asynchronies, space itself becomes the marker of time –
a singular time, identical only with itself, that is, identical with
its place in a global continuum of capital-space. Of course, such
a definition of time and space would be tautological.

VI.

In capitalism, however, the dialectic of time and space is uneven,
asymmetric, and ultimately stretched into a dead eternity. In
credit-based, and therefore debt-driven economies, space is
not simply another extension of time beyond present, past, and
future. Today's profit has its future origin in the extraction of a

certain "amount" of abstract labour-time. The retroactive time of capital is speculative by definition. In this way, capital bets on a future to which it is irredeemably indebted. Given the incalculable "amount" of future abstract labour-time that is valorized in today's capitalism, the time of the future is not anymore "our" future. Rather, the future of capital time already owns us and we owe to a future without history. The financialization of capitalism presents the last, most radical stage of this basic dynamic. There is no future redemption in the economy of debt, only the uncertain promise to remain "credible" – to believe in the "credo of capital" (C I, 919). Under these conditions, time is not a neutral measure of spatial difference like chronometric time, but a speculative resource that temporalizes itself through the exploitation of labour-power.

The more undead labour is forced to spin the time of real abstraction, the less the time of capital will ever arrive at historical time. Capital's totalizing ontology, woven out of a tautological self-identical time, leaves no indeterminate empty spots, no undefinable gaps of time which could become undefined openings to a non-capitalist future. Against the sensuous supra-sensuous reality of undead returns and self-identical "now-time," Benjamin insisted on a heterogeneous temporality of "now-time" – an anachronic constellation of past and present shot through with sparks of "messianic" time.[16] Without these anachronic short-circuits and messianic gaps, historical time would lose its historical character. For Benjamin, history is thus incomplete in a radical sense – its texture is woven of struggles, catastrophes, and failures – and it can therefore never be self-temporalizing, self-sufficient or identical with itself. The inaccessible wheel of history does not spin the yarn of abstract labour, it only weaves holes into the cloth of capital time. The fragmentary work of holes sets free the whole of undead labour – it weaves a contingent, heterogeneous, discontinuous cloth. History is nothing other than this negative spin, unbound.

16 Walter Benjamin, "On the Concept of History", p. 395.

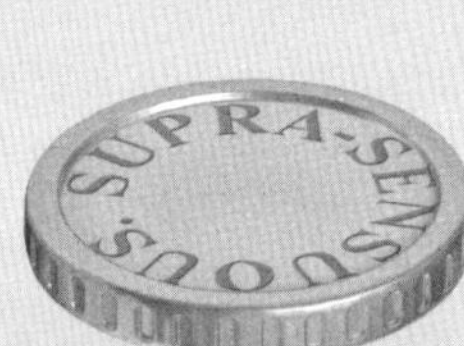

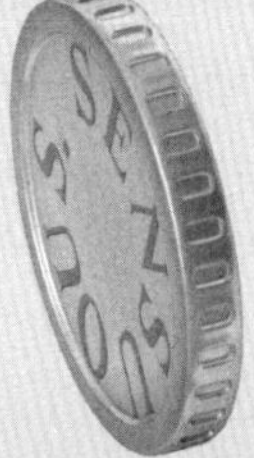

Zachary Formwalt

SCHÄUBLE AND THE CRITIQUE OF POLITICAL ECONOMY

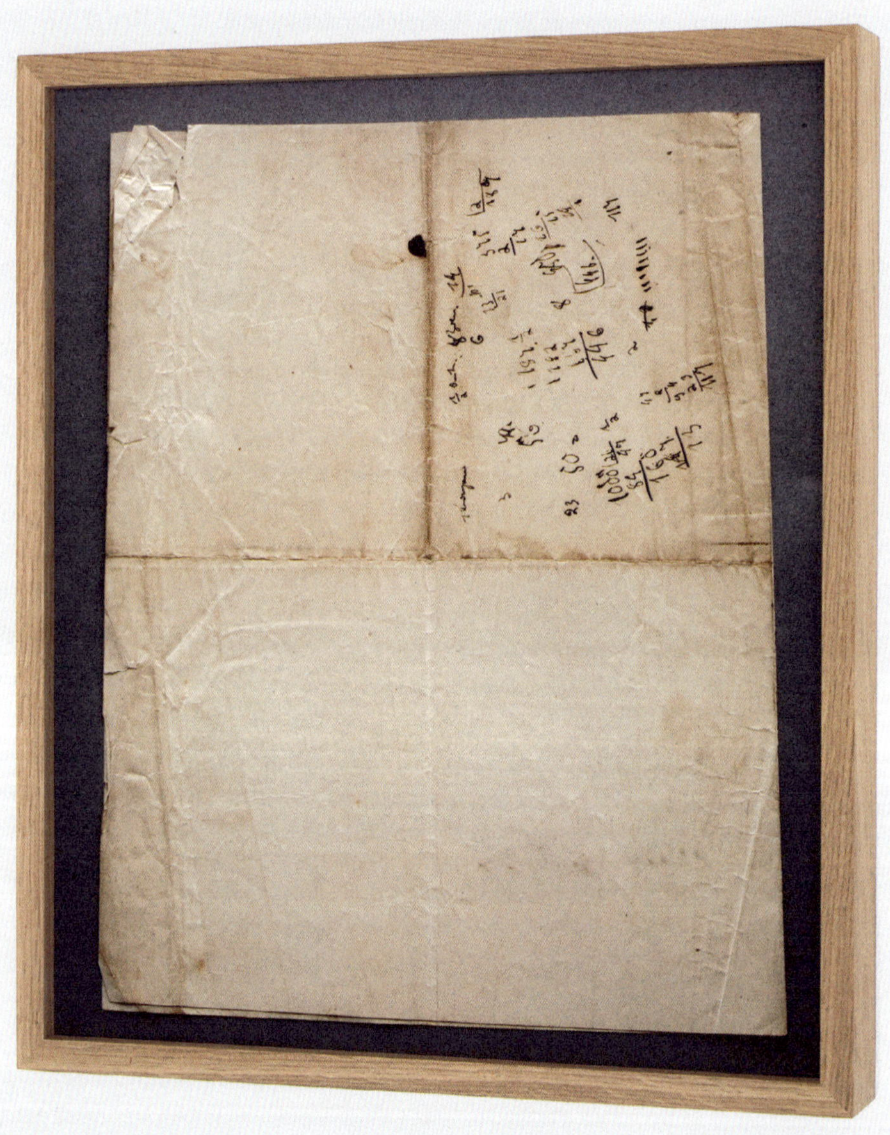

Am 14.01.2016 um 13:47 schrieb Zachary Formwalt:

Hi M,
I have a couple of questions:
Is the title "Gutes Böses Geld" a working title or the final
exhibition title?
And when is the opening?

Thanks!
Zachary

Am 14.01.2016 um 13:59 schrieb Zachary Formwalt:

Hi M,

I have one other question which comes instead of these other
two that I just found the answer to on the Kunsthalle's website:
What does it mean that "Dr. Wolfgang Schäuble, German Federal
Minister of Finances, is the patron of the exhibition"?

best,
zachary

Am 15.01.2016 um 13:45 schrieb Zachary Formwalt:

Dear M,

Thank you for the invitation to come to the opening. It would indeed be nice to meet and I would like to see the exhibition.

I understand that the Staatliche Kunsthalle is a state-sponsored institution, and is thus vulnerable to a certain kind of embrace by politicians active in government. An exhibition such as this, which focuses on the theme of money, seems a natural fit for the minister of finance. But I find this public endorsement/embrace highly problematic to the extent that it suggests a very real inability on the part of the work within it to effectively question the views held and actions taken by this particular minister of finance, Wolfgang Schäuble. One of the great advantages of state-sponsored institutions in my opinion is that their primary support comes from a democratically elected body. When a particular member of this body supports an institution, I think that is different, and it requires a bit more scrutiny of said individual.

I can imagine some works that would withstand the embrace of Schäuble, but I don't think that *Kritik der Politik und Nationalökonomie* is one of them. It is a work that is very sensitive to the context in which it is presented. I wasn't aware of this particular element of that context until yesterday. Now that I am I feel that I must decline the invitation to show *Kritik der Politik und Nationalökonomie* within it.

all the best,
zachary

January 15, 2016

Just off the phone with M from Staatliche Kunsthalle Baden-
Baden regarding my pulling out of the show due to the public
support the show is receiving from Wolfgang Schäuble. Emailed
with Sven L. earlier today, asking him what he knew about
this patronage situation. He gave a great summary of the
Schirmherrschaft situation in Germany. He seemed pretty sure
that it was someone at the Kunsthalle who approached Schäuble
and not vice-versa. It turns out that it is vice-versa! Elections
will take place two or three weeks after the show opens and
Schäuble wanted to be visible to help win in these elections. M
claims that it happens that usually it is lower local politicians
but the big federal ones can bump them if they so desire. Rest of
the Kunsthalle staff not in favour of this and it came at the last
minute so they are worried about losing any kind of critical edge.
About their show losing the work that would in a way undermine
Schäuble. It's definitely more interesting this way. Should the
Kunsthalle be buttressed against this last minute hijack? But how
does one do this? Pulling out publicly is one option. But how to
stay in and do something to address the situation and Schäuble
as directly as possible?

I asked for the weekend to think about whether or not to stay in.

January 18, 2016

First draft of an open letter addressed to Schäuble and hung
alongside the photograph of the Marx contract.

> Dear Dr. Schäuble,
>
> I am writing you this letter in case you come to see this
> exhibition of which you are the patron. But of course, as an
> open letter, I am also writing it, perhaps even primarily, for
> the others who come to see the exhibition. When I first agreed
> to loan the piece *Kritik der Politik und Nationalökonomie,*

I was unaware that you would have anything to do with the exhibition and when I found out that you would be listed as the patron, I immediately felt that this might affect the artwork in question. So a new condition had to be added to the loan. The exhibition of this letter alongside *Kritik der Politik und Nationalökonomie* is that new condition.

The title of the work comes from a contract that Karl Marx signed with the publisher Carl Leske, in 1845. The contract was unfulfilled. Marx did not deliver the *Kritik der Politik und Nationalökonomie* manuscript to Leske. The money advanced to Marx by Leske with this contract would not bear the fruit he had intended. I have taken the title of this work for the photograph you see here, of an old sheet of paper that has been folded twice so that it is divided into quadrants. On one of these quadrants a series of numbers has been written, simple sums worked out. Perhaps a quick set of calculations related to Marx's personal economy (it is his copy of the contract). Or perhaps they are something more, related, perhaps, to the *wissenschaftich* investigation for which Leske was asking and that Marx would eventually produce, though with a different publisher and a slightly different title. There is an ambiguity in any case. We don't know what the numbers refer to. It could be expenses, debts balanced against income, or something else entirely. It's hard not to see it as some form of money in any case.

Though Marx did not deliver the manuscript to Leske, he did work on it. This work would not be published until 1932, long after both Marx and Leske had died. The work took the form of a set of manuscripts that came to be referred to as the *Economic and Philosophic Manuscripts of 1844*. The description of alienated labor and its relation to private property in the manuscripts is famous. But there is also a small section on money [*Geld*]. It was this section that I was really thinking about when making the *Kritik der Politik und Nationalökonomie*. In particular there is an interesting definition of money that Marx puts forward, as "the external common medium for turning an image [*Vorstellung*] into reality [*Wirklichkeit*] and reality into a mere image." As you can see the English translator has taken liberties with

the German *Vorstellung*, rendering something immediately
resonant to a visual artist such as myself.

When I think of the negotiations with Greece in which you
played such a prominent role, one of the first things that
comes to mind is precisely such a medium of exchange
between image and reality. But it's not money that I think
of, it's the dissolution of real material things, big things, like
buildings, airports, railways and utilities. Things that are
often at least partially owned by the state. Things which the
Greek state was pressured into selling in order to pay back the
banks which had loaned them the money they no longer had.
These big things could be turned into money and the accounts
could be balanced. But what then would happen to these
things? After the medium has turned reality into an image,
the medium doesn't disappear, it simply turns the image—the
representation, the quantity now owned by someone—back
into reality.

Of course this is a simplification, but sometimes a
simplification is needed to understand again how something
which has become so complex in its own register, relates
to a world of which it is a part. When figures enter into the
billions, it's hard to remember that, and to imagine how, these
numbers relate to actual everyday people, working out their
personal finances on scraps of paper, or spreadsheets, as
the case may be. It's this relation, that should be organized
democratically, with all of the problems that entails. When
people understand that the current economic system is no
longer working because it does not allow them and their
communities to live in a way that they find acceptable,
a medium should be available for them to express this
understanding and make changes to the economic system.
At certain historical conjunctures, this simple reminder
might serve as well as a three or four volume work on
political economy.

Not sure how exactly to end this. And there is something
interesting left out here with the Prussian censorship issue in the
Marx/Leske correspondence. Pick it up tomorrow.

19 January 2016

On the censorship issue ended with yesterday: Carl Leske expresses concern over the political nature of Marx's *Kritik der Politik und Nationalökonomie*. He says Marx should keep it *rein wissenschaftlich* in order to prevent its censorship or worse by the Prussian authorities. Marx drafts a letter in response to Leske's letters where he first assures him that the work would indeed be scientific, though perhaps not in the way that the Prussian authorities think of this term, and then assures him that he is looking for another publisher. He then continues:

On the other hand you will recall that in Paris, as in the written contract, nothing was agreed about how revolutionary the form of the work was to be, and that, on the contrary, I even believed it necessary at the time to bring out both volumes simultaneously, because the publication of the first volume would entail the banning or confiscation of the second.

This opposition of "revolutionary form to scientific form, or political to academic: Keep it scientific! Keep it academic!" i.e., don't appear to question the presuppositions, the conditions, of science and/or academia, which, implicitly, operate at the pleasure of the authorities. Scientific/academic form here appears as the form of exposition of the ruling class, the hegemon. Crucially, these are the forms of the objective, or at least of objective investigation, in a given situation. Keeping it scientific will keep it uncensored. Or rather, the scientific form carries the censorship within it.

But this is precisely what science was not, at least in the way that Marx would grapple with it from that first critique of political economy that Leske was initially to publish, up to his last critique of political economy, *Capital*. The science of political economy was a critical endeavor which would, precisely, question the presuppositions of classical economics, that supposed science which fails to see the social relations of production which condition all of the elements taken as primary in classical economy. These elements appearing in the field of reality [*Wirklichkeit*] are only elemental to the perception of (or, from the POV of) individuals in that field. It's where science *could* begin. But this would be a science that cracks the censorship programmed into the field of appearances.

So, how is this relevant to an exhibition with the subtitle, 'a visual history of the economy' which, it turns out, is under the patronage of Wolfgang Schäuble?

Regarding the need to adapt the form of expression in order to evade censorship:

Here there is a kind of inversion. The work having already been made and then included in an exhibition, its form is not altered to evade any kind of censorship. Rather, a particularly well-known and effective politician implementing extreme austerity measures in the EU decides to attach his name to this exhibition thus approving on some level whatever is appearing there. Any kind of opposing or critical stance toward this politician's positions and actions is rendered acceptable to said politician. Or to put it more bluntly, it is rendered powerless, ineffective. Instead of the imperative of clothing one's critique in the jargon of science, or in this case, in the terms of neoliberal economic policy (austerity, structural reform, budget surplus, etc.), one is presented with the request: *submit your critique and we will embrace it as inconsequential.*

One could of course address the situation directly via some kind of supplement to the work, as it hasn't been shipped yet. I still have it in my possession and with that comes some control at the moment. Once they have it, who knows what five lines Schäuble will write in the catalogue. Probably some moralizing about how one should use money responsibly. He will of course cloak his austerity agenda in the terms of responsibility and moderation. As one of the purer specimens of neoliberal politician, he will certainly avoid the term "neoliberal" altogether.

But to the point, he is using the opportunity in relation to the forthcoming elections. Of course whether this photograph of the backside of a contract that Marx signed in 1845 is in the show or not won't make a bit of difference in that. In this respect there is no tactic that I can see that would achieve anything immediately. But perhaps this is an opportunity to deal with

something that crops up more and more these days, which is
the problem of sponsorship in general, though this is usually
to do with corporate sponsors. Here the situation is somewhat
unique because you have a real ideological figurehead, rather
than some corporate sponsor who turns out to be involved in war
crimes committed while extracting oil in Nigeria (Shell) or Sudan
(Lundin), for example.

January 20, 2016

Internet search on Schäuble on the one hand turns up
a little video from the Politics section of the *Bild* website, of
Schäuble presenting a new postage stamp honoring Axel
Springer (a former journalist and founder of the Axel Springer SE
publishing corporation).

On the other hand, re-reading Marx's 1857 introduction to the
Grundrisse turns up this quote at the end: "What chance has
Hermes against the *Crédit Mobilier*?"

Continuing the internet search, here is the first part of the entry
for *Crédit Mobilier* in Wikipedia:

*Crédit Mobilier (officially the Société Générale du Crédit Mobilier)
was a French banking company, and one of the most important
financial institutions of the world during the mid-19th century.
It had a major role in the financing of numerous railroads and
other infrastructure projects by mobilizing the savings of middle
class French investors as capital for vast lending schemes.*
***The Crédit Mobilier investments created vast debts for the
countries which accepted these infrastructure loans*** *and
was thus indirectly involved in the European occupations of the
countries whose governments defaulted on these loans during
the worldwide economic depression of the 1870s.*

Hard not to see a kind of precedent here in relation to the capital
that poured into Greece and the other "PIGS" (Portugal, Ireland
and Spain), after the introduction of the Euro. Followed up by
"structural adjustment" to then service that debt.

Sure enough, Hermes is the symbol of ELTA, the Hellenic Post, one of the many state assets that are being sold off to go into this 50 billion euro fund proposed by Schäuble during the negotiations with Greece after the referendum last summer.

The Hermes-motif goes back to the very beginning of Greek postage stamps, with the first designs referred to as the "Large Hermes Heads."

It turns out that the same plates were used for the first twenty-five years of printing, from 1861 all the way up until 1886. These stamps are legendary for this reason. The only way that one can distinguish between the different series is through an inspection of the quality of the printing, how worn out the plates were when the stamp in question was printed, the paper on which it was printed varies in some years, and the plates were sometimes cleaned, sometimes not in certain print years. And of course the inks varied somewhat in different series. All these material factors condition the reproduction of the same image as an incarnation of postal value.

Instead of a planned intelligibility of philatelic moments expressed through details in stamp design, there is instead a series of material facts, fallout from printing events which would later be analyzed and categorized to produce a history of early Greek postage stamps.

Marx writes in the introduction of the *Grundrisse* manuscript:

The so-called historical presentation of development is founded, as a rule, on the fact that the latest form regards the previous ones as steps leading up to itself, and, since it is only rarely and only under quite specific conditions able to criticize itself – leaving aside, of course, the historical periods which appear to themselves as times of decadence—it always conceives them one-sidedly.

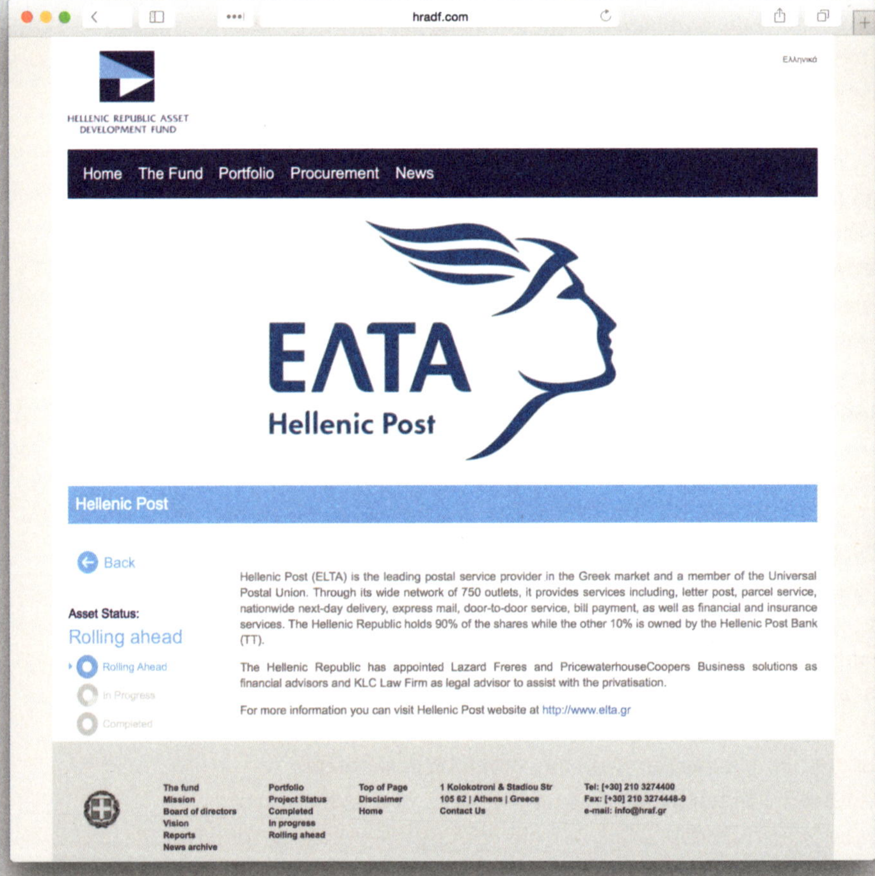

January 24, 2016

Back to censorship and the exhibition:

Anything that would *directly* address the situation with Schäuble and the *Schirmherrschaft* system in an accompanying text would not, I think, be allowed and in any case, it wouldn't be very effective. Schäuble is using the situation just to have his name out there during the election period. The question is more about the broader problem of sponsorship in the arts. The exhibition itself seems like it could be interesting. There are works by other artists for whom I have great respect and the context is a good one. But that catalogue will probably be a real disaster. I dread reading the Schäuble text, though it will certainly be the first thing I do when I get my hands on it! Here again, it would then be about publishing something in another venue that might be able to address the whole situation.

So I mailed M to tell him that I'd just let the piece stay in as is and mentioned that I was working now on a kind of supplement in the form of the Hermes stamp project, but it wasn't something that would anyway be ready in time.

January 27, 2016

New Hermes stamps arrived!

The metallic Flying Hermes stamps from 1901 are amazing when scanned. The black one is defined at every level in the printing. But the silver and gold ones have an ephemeral quality at certain points. For example, the feet disappear, or the pointing finger. But especially where the foot meets the figure blowing up from below. Imagine just reading sections of these—a whole series of fragments across the inks. The same design, but different parts do different things in different ink.

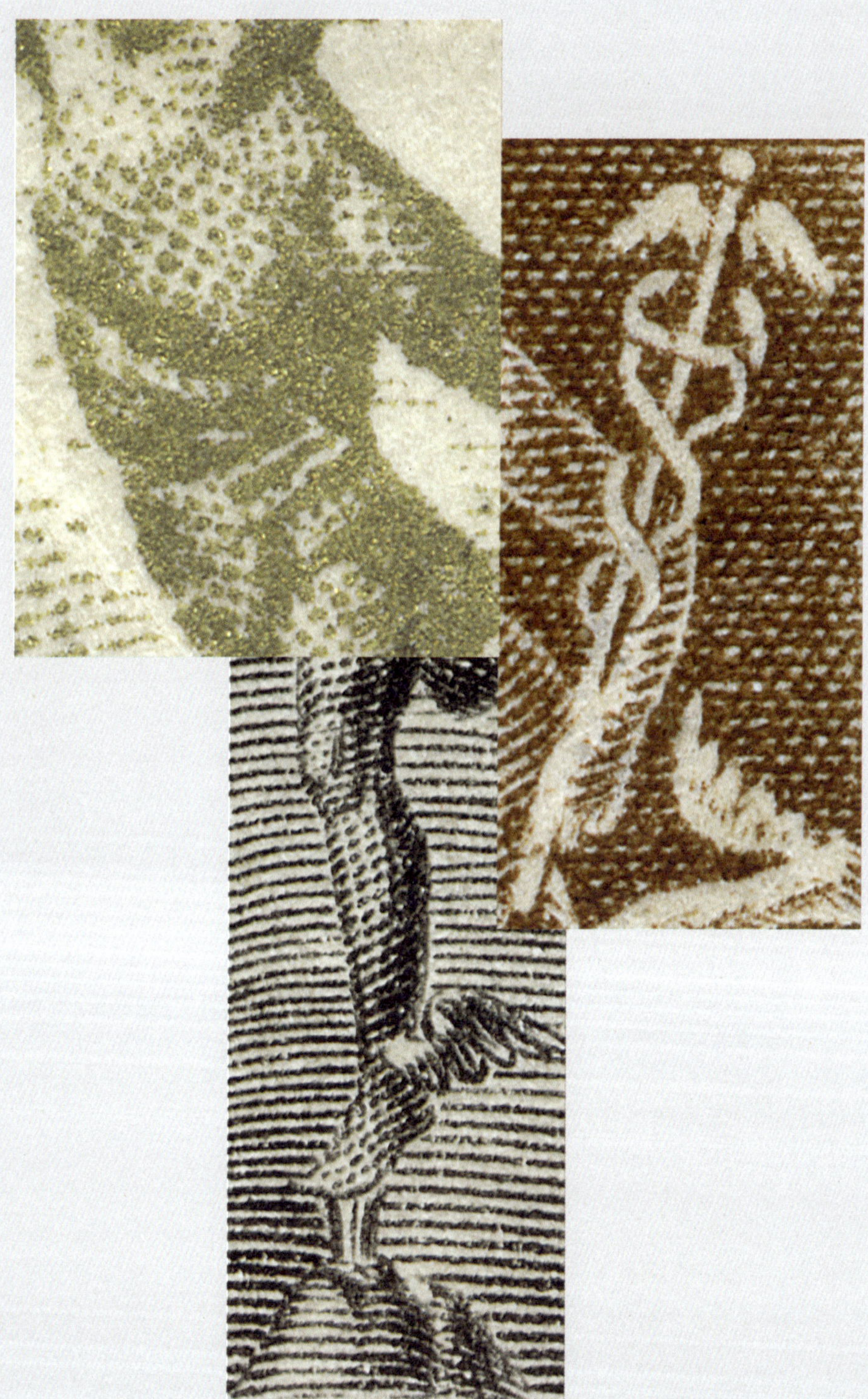

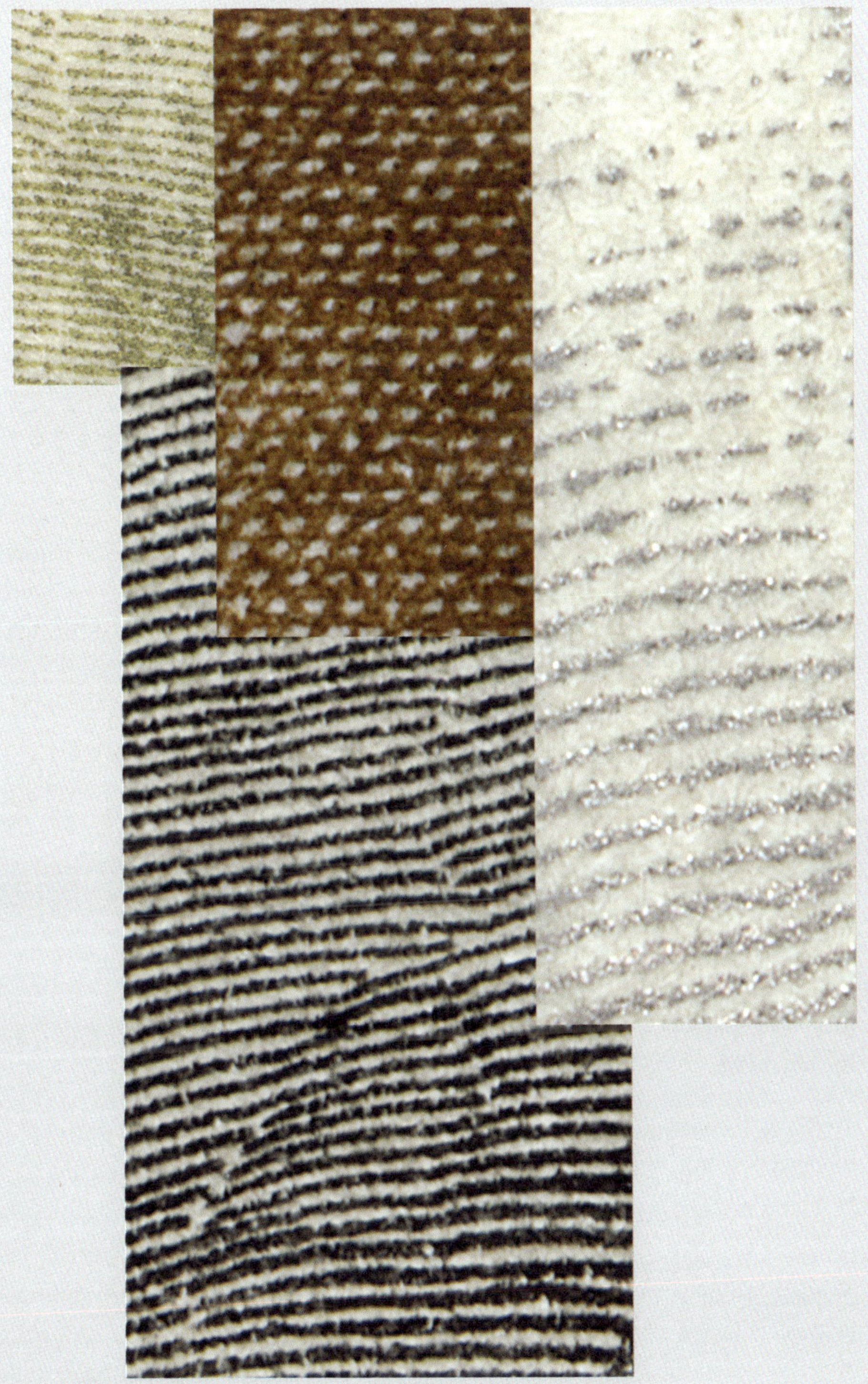

Also, this breakup of a single entity—a single image/design—
into a number of different components which cannot be easily
put back together just by looking at them. They don't construct
a whole when put back together because they come from
different inks, different values (numbers and denominations)
and different prints. In any case, the relation of this breakup
into parts and the putting it back together into some kind of
Frankenstein that no longer relates back to the original could
serve as an allegory of the way in which securitization works, or
simply the privatization (breakup and sale on the market) that
the Greek postal service among many other "assets" must now
undergo. This kind of material dissolution or breakup should be
carried out especially with the stamps printed in metallic inks.
What becomes of Hermes after the HRADF (Hellenic Republic
Asset Development Fund)?

Perhaps one progression should be kept. The blue Hermes heads
up until the AM prints (*Axia Metalliki* = Metal Value, i.e. in gold
at this time). These were made in 1900-1901, when the drachma
had gone down dramatically in value, to be used on packages
and for foreign money orders.

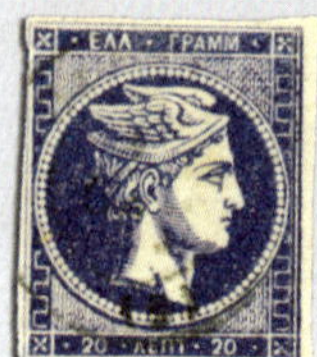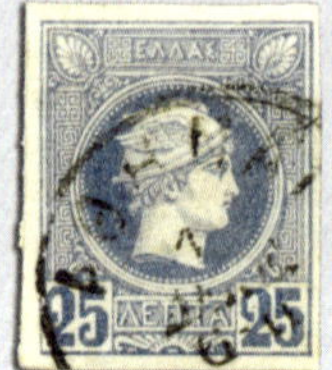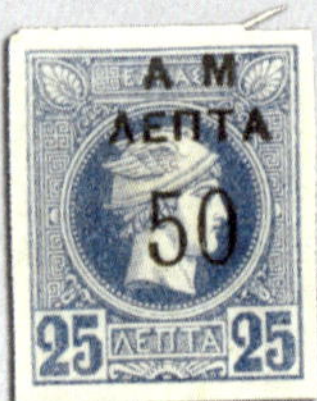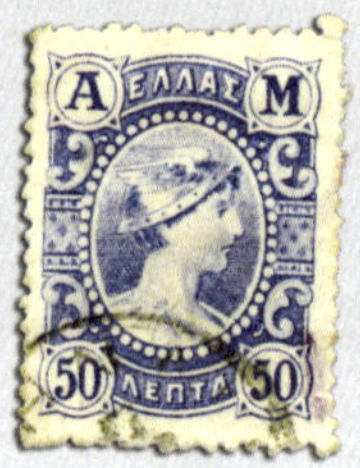

The whole history of the **Latin Monetary Union** should
be looked at in relation to the Euro, including especially
the following:

1) The decline in the value of silver due to technological
innovation in mining techniques. The image of technological
development behind which a number of brutal production
realities lie.

2) The story about German traders exploiting the difference
between gold and silver prices by bringing silver into the Latin

Monetary Union to be minted at rates above its value and then exchanging this for gold. It is a better story about the motivation behind keeping inflation low in contemporary Germany than the tired one about Weimar-era hyperinflation leading to Hitler. This would be more about an economic strategy than a fear of repeating a terrible episode in history. Why it benefits German capital to keep wages artificially low there, thus increasing their competitiveness in exports. German banks make loans to Greece (i.e. they send their silver) in order to get back gold in the form of the assets sold off by the Greek state in order to pay for the worthless silver.

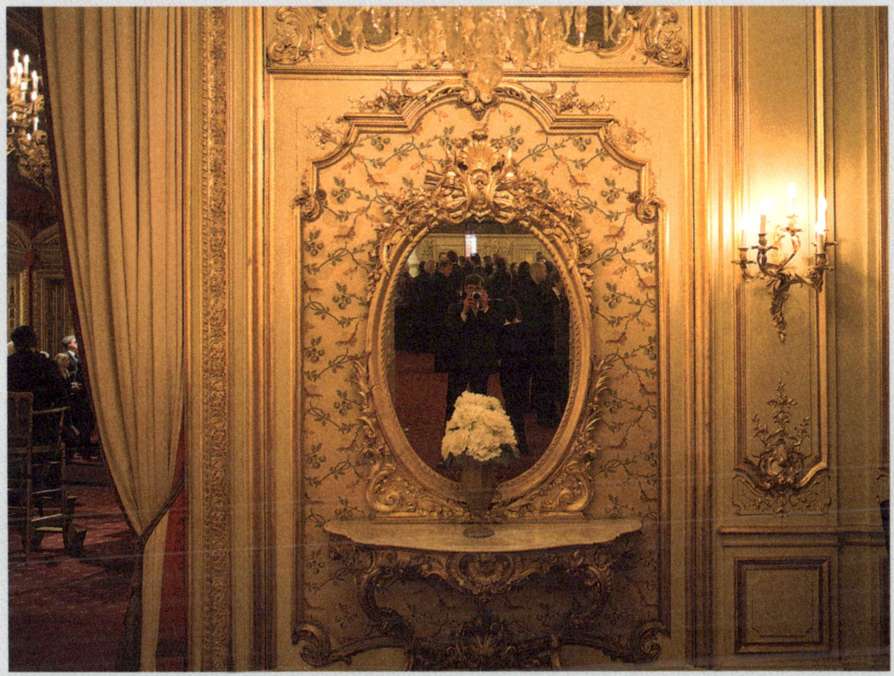

March 5, 2016

Last night was the opening at Kunsthalle Baden-Baden. Part of the exhibition is actually in the casino, where there were drinks after the speeches and such in the Kunsthalle. Awkward entrance to the casino involved being suited up in a ridiculous suit coat that was much too big.

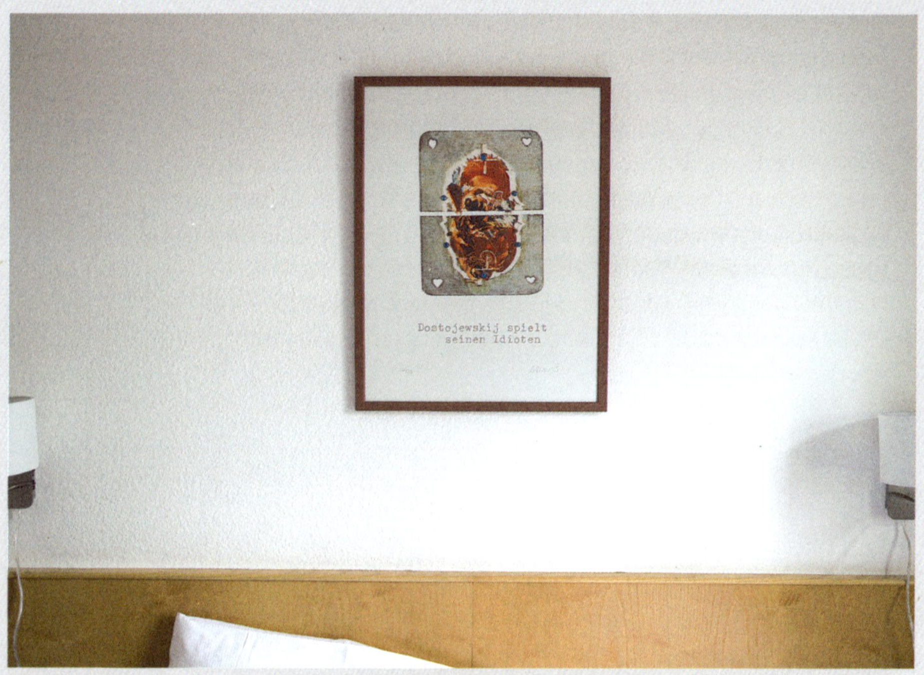

Shortly thereafter I was rather politely asked to put away my camera. This was a casino after all and as people are quick to tell you here, it's where Dostoyevsky wrote *The Gambler*, in order, supposedly, to pay off his own gambling debts.

Even the hotel artwork above my bed took part in this—*Dostojewskij spielt seinen Idioten*.

At the Kunsthalle portion of the opening I caught a glimpse of the catalogue proof. I immediately looked for Schäuble's text, and quickly photographed it so I could read through it again later.

As predicted, Schäuble moralizes on the issue of money. That he would literally quote his own sermon though... that I hadn't seen coming!

[I]n a political sermon on the question of "Cleverly Dealing with Mammon?" […] I argued against a certain moral superiority with which Christians often make things too easy for themselves when it comes to money. No, the issue is how we approach

money. Treating it as a limited resource: not exaggerating with creating money from nothing, something that Goethe already saw critically in Faust II, where the Emperor directly demands: "Money is lacking. Well, then make some!"; not allowing money to send the wrong signals to individuals or to governments to act unreasonably or irresponsibly by insuring that the consequences of financial decisions are ultimately also borne by those who made these decisions—all this has nothing to do with the oft-bemoaned "neoliberal economization" of our society, but is simply unwise.

On the way over to the Casino for further opening festivities; I spoke with a couple of other artists in the show about the Schäuble situation. They too were not particularly happy about it, but had not considered pulling out because that principle implied the impossibility of exhibiting anywhere considering funding sources these days. *But with such a well-known figure as Wolfgang Schäuble, wasn't it different?* Not really, was the answer, and what would pulling out accomplish anyway? Better to offer up an opposing worldview than to simply refuse. Which is of course part of the problem. The refusal must be registered and made to resonate. To quietly refuse doesn't accomplish anything. One must do something else instead. And here one ends up very quickly with questions of agency within an art practice.

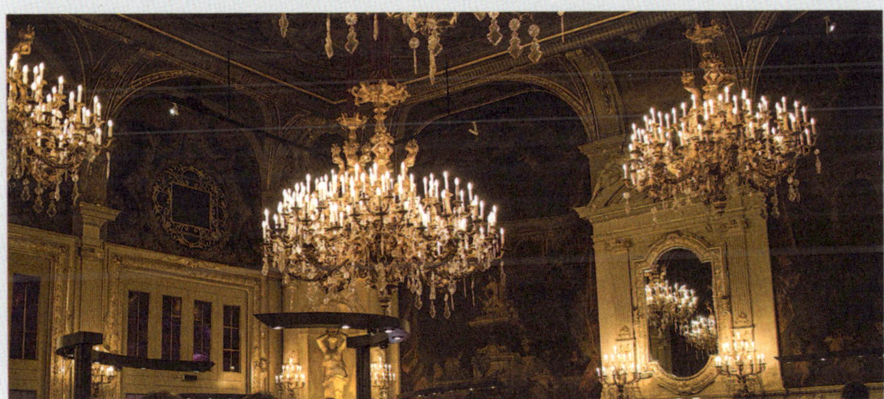

As we approached the casino, I thought about Schäuble's sermon on the clever usage of mammon. And his quick dismissal of the term "neoliberal" in exchange for "wisdom": The "oft-bemoaned" austerity agenda need not be referred to as "neoliberal

economization" when it can more simply be described as wise
economic policy. It was a lot more propagandistic than I had
expected, those five lines of Schäuble's.

May 24, 2016

Just received the catalog for *Money, Good and Evil. A Visual
History of the Economy*. A couple of changes were made in the
English version of Schäuble's text. The key term, "wisdom"
was changed to "prudence." So now it is prudence that should
be substituted for neoliberal economization. Prudence, wisdom,
austerity, neoliberal economization, call it what you will
Wolfgang Schäuble, it's still the political project of impoverishing
the vast majority of the global population in order to uphold
a rather strange idea of money as something other than
a social relation.

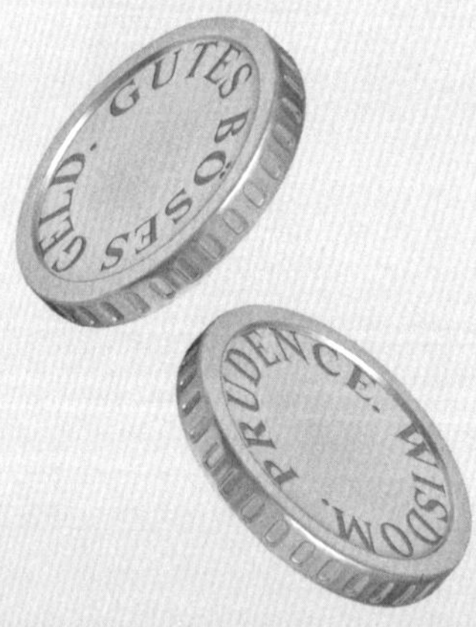

FOLLOWING PAGES

→

Antonis Pittas
ON COLOUR THEORY

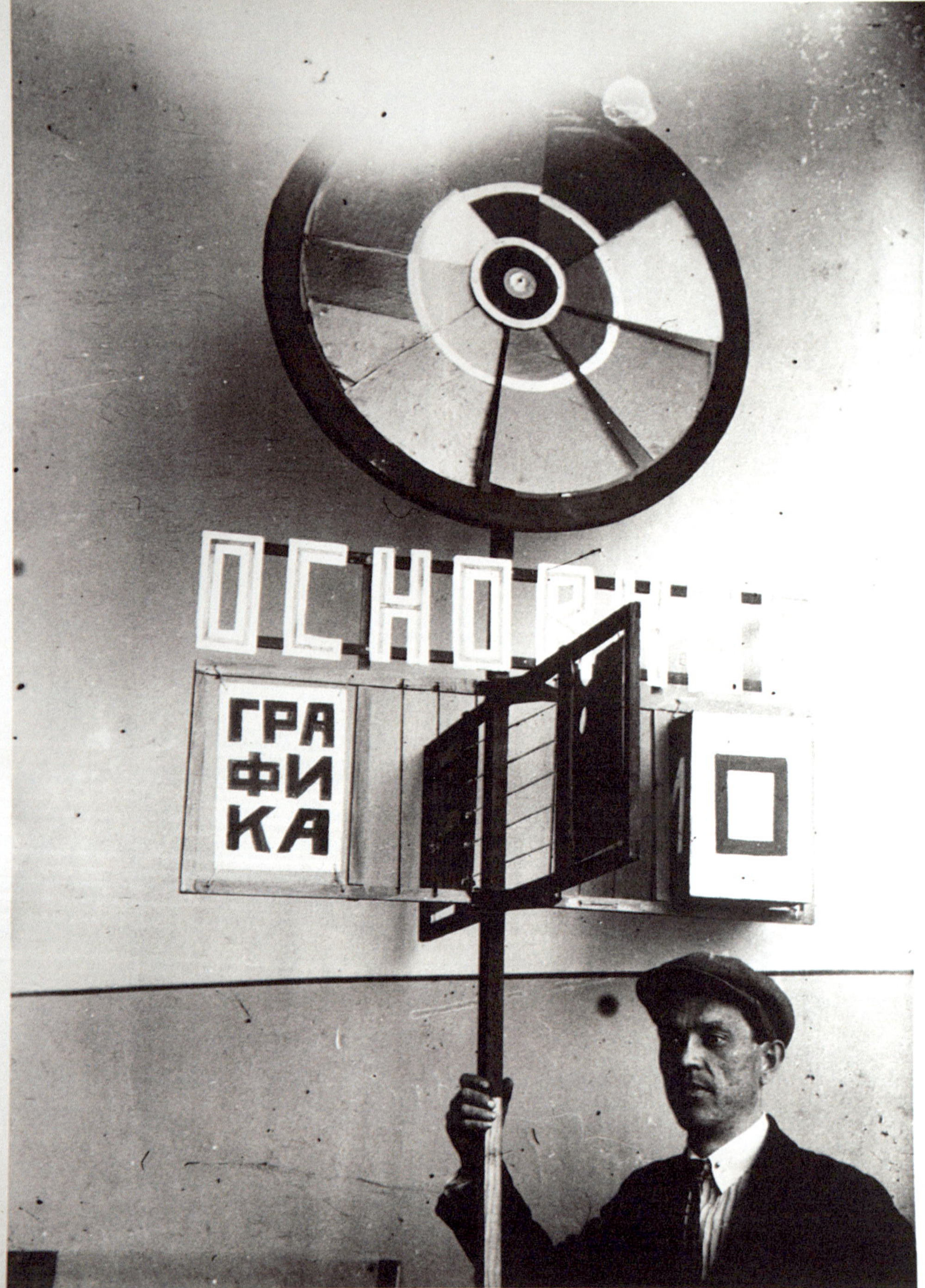
ОСНО
ГРА
ФИ
КА
О

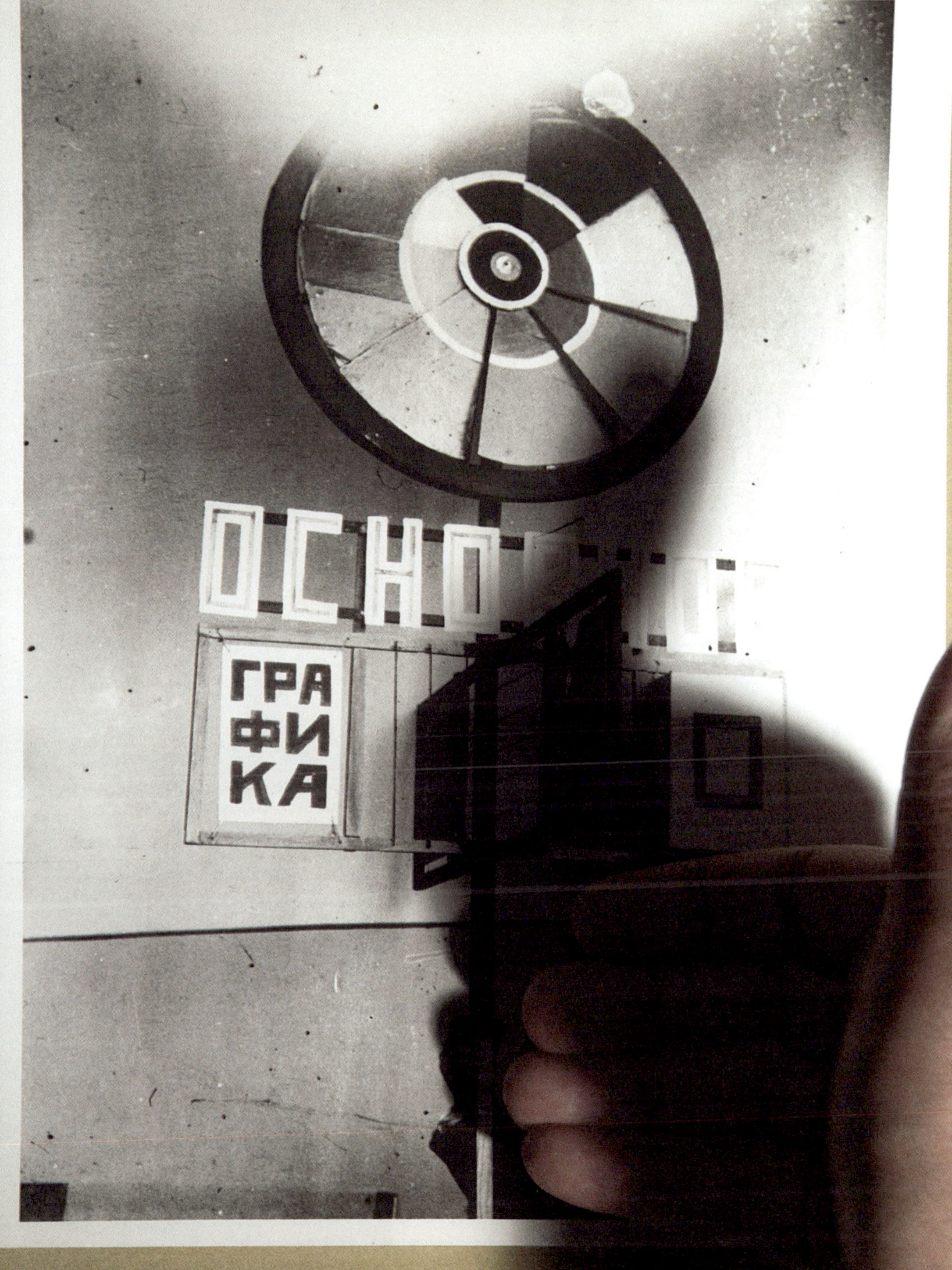
ОСНО
ГРА
ФИ
КА

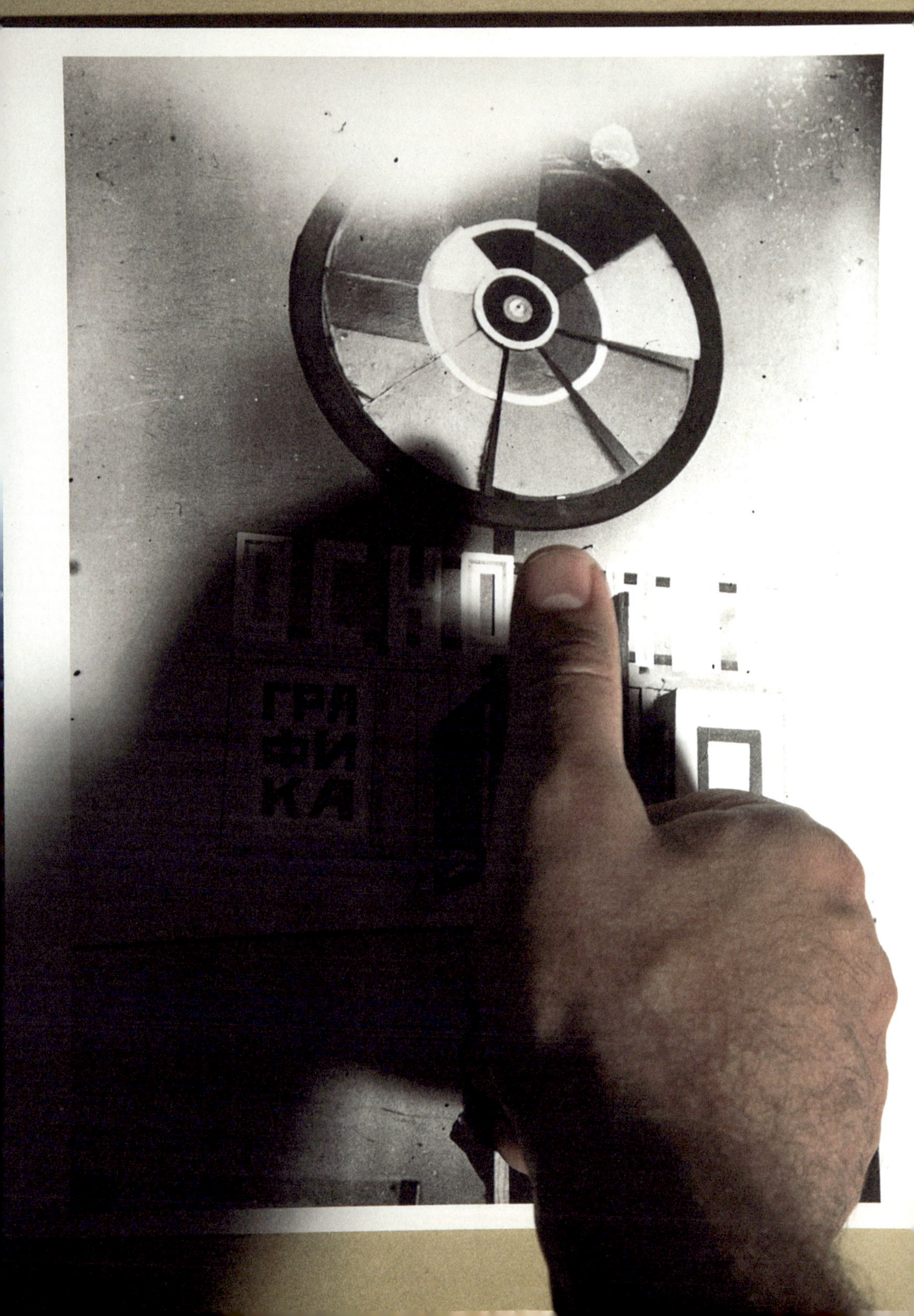
ГРА
ФИ
КА

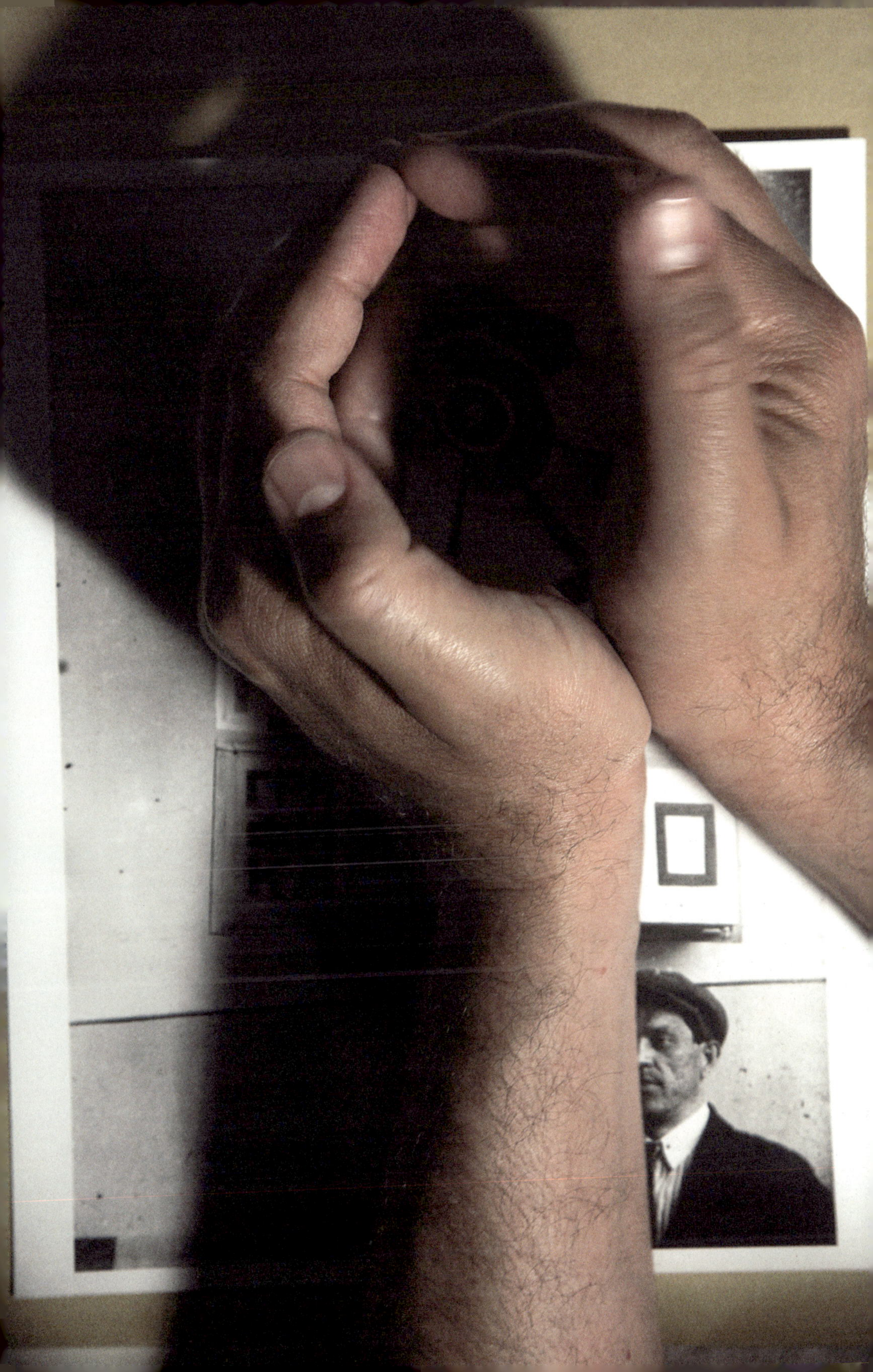

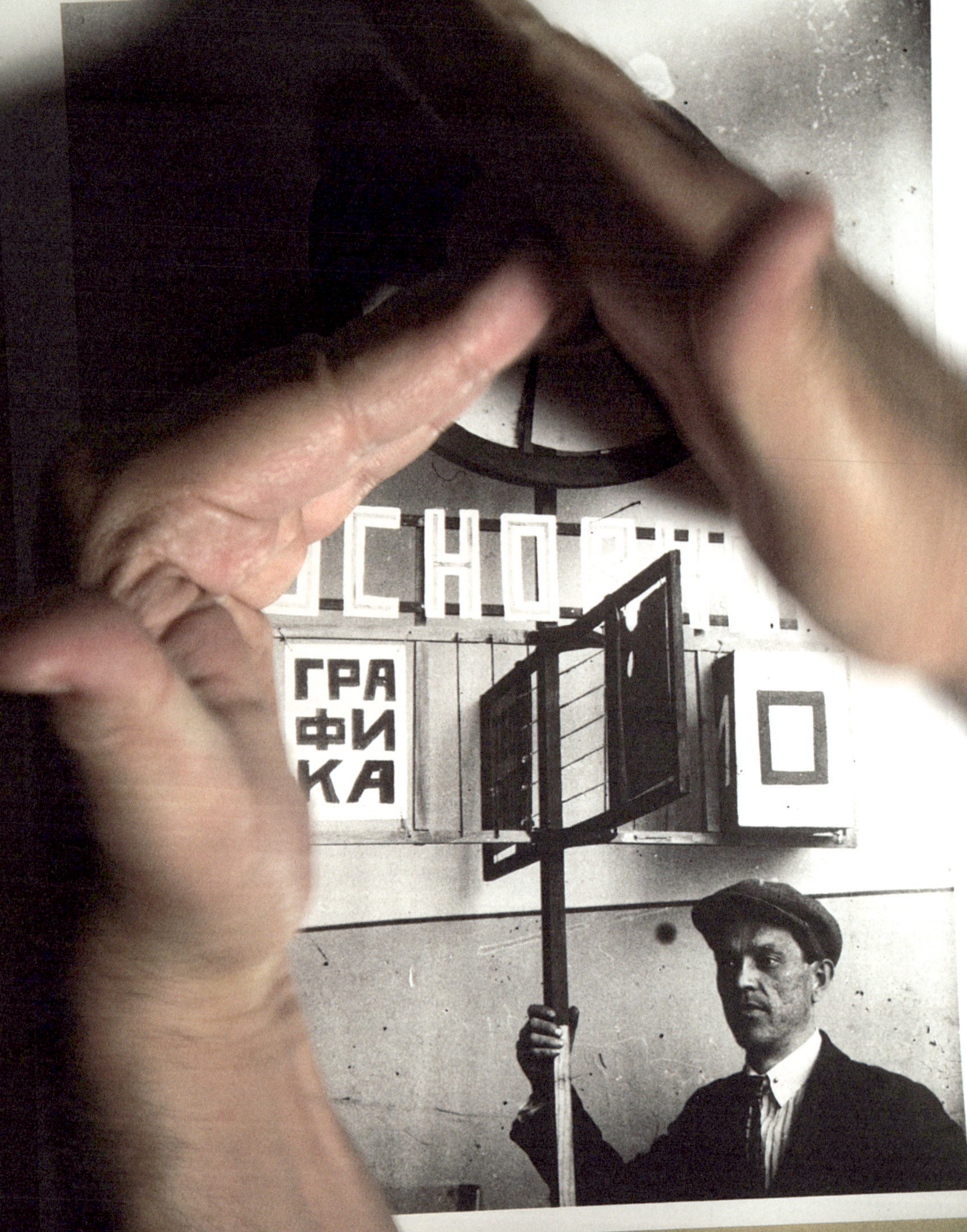
СНО
ГРА
ФИ
КА
О

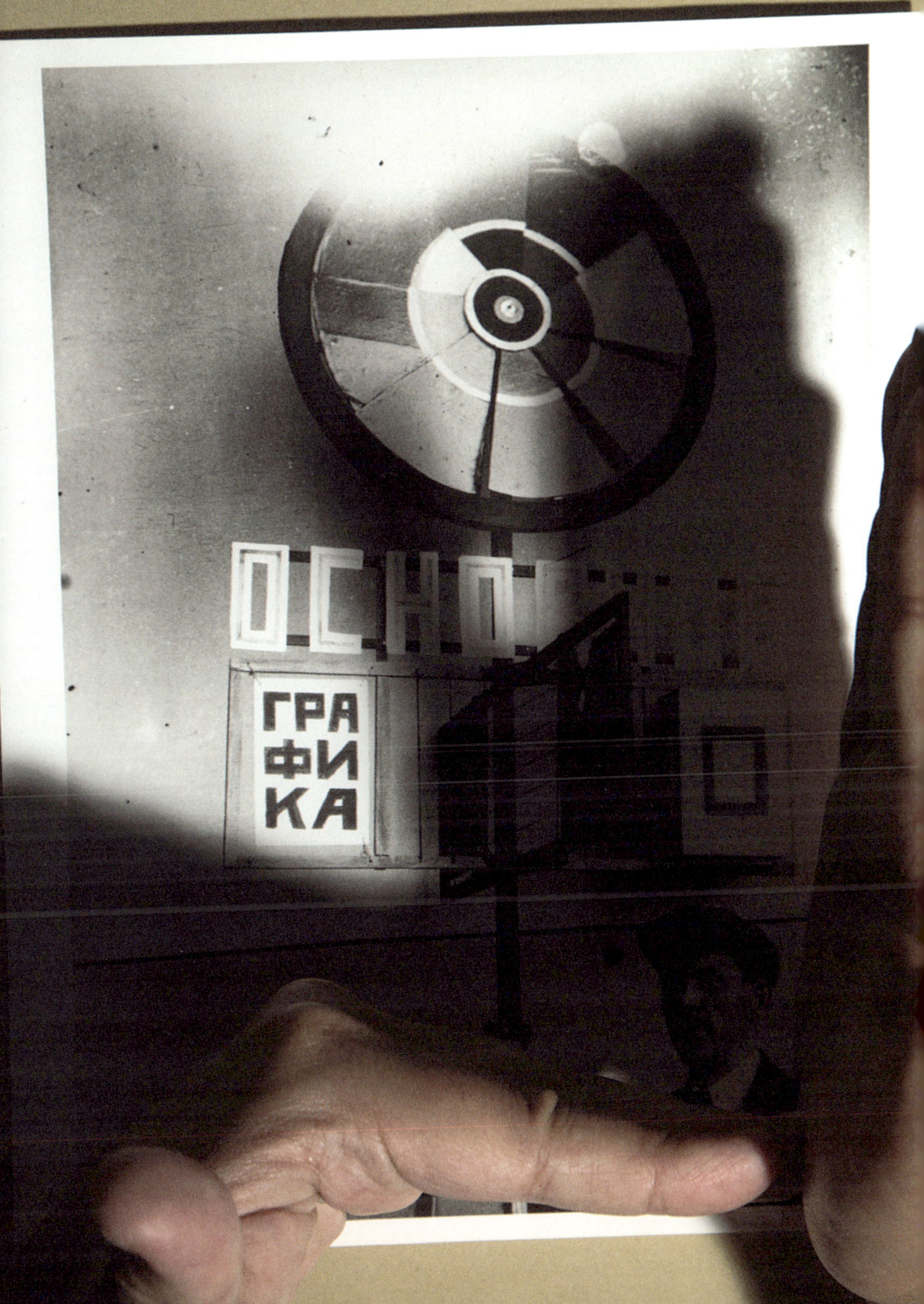
ОСНО
ГРА
ФИ
КА

From: **Helen Wong** i0am0mrs0helen0wong@yahoo.co.uk
Subject: We need to discuss, as discussed
Date: 2 Apr 2015 12:05
To:

Great Greetings,

I am Mrs Helen Wong from General Federal Bank of Kerching. You might not believe it, but please do.

Up until recently I was a happy chicken flying on wings of promises, but since the beginning of this year my life has fallen down between the cracks of bad fortune. My husband, the former CEO of the General Federal Bank of Kerching left me for a younger swan that he met upon the lakes of love. Due to this shameful rejection, he forced me to go underground. You might not see it, but whenever a coin falls through a crack, I am ready to pick it up before it reaches the bottom. My hands are soar and thinly worn from the toils of coin-picking in urban cracks and holes. This is why I write to you, my golden bean.

The day my husband denounced me, I withdrew $ 500 000 000 000 000 000 000 000 000 000 000 000 000 000 000 000 000 000 from his account which was still within my reach before the door his warm door was shut upon my forehead. I am now hiding here between the cracks in the ground, you can not see me, but please do, and please understand that I am willing to give you this fortune of $ 500 000 000 000 000 000 000 000 000 000 000 000 000 000 000 000 000 000 000 if you pull me out of the ground in time.

In exchange, my wish is that you donate a mere $ 500 to the General Federal Bank of Kerching As Ap As Possible, as the cracks that I call home are about to be filled by pidgeons feathers as well as steaming concrete from the expanding real-estates in this wealthy area.

Yes is nothing but a number, so please say it twice.

Yours Sensory,
Mrs Helen Wong

From: **Helen Wong** i0am0mrs0helen0wong@yahoo.co.uk
Subject: Be Bup be bep, as beaped
Date: 14 Apr 2015 20:52
To:

Beap Buppeti,

Ba beb Mrs Helen Wong beap General Federal Bank of Kerching. Bup Beap bip beap bipi, bup beap ba.

B bea Be bup buppeb bi ba bip b lifestory, bipp ba bea bup bippibup bu fortune bp, be bup buppeb bip!! Bippi! Bippebi buo bup bip buppibap bup yourself.

Bip! Buppebu bip bup be bup be be be bebe life be bup bi bup bip bap bap beppi. Beppi bup fortunate Mr. Wong beap bu bee be bupp bap bip bu bab bb bup up bu buu beppeppeppebab death. B be beap beeppippepb bu bepi bi pi eb bep bupe pep bbbbb ipb bap $ 500 000 000 000 000 000 000 000 000 000 000 000 000 000 000 000 000 000 000 000 bu up ppibb abb babb ab. Bei bu bebbibapp pabbibeb be bu unhappy.

Be babba abb pep ap be baeap apa bapp bip you! Beppi trust bep bep $ 500 bi pib General Federal Bank of Kerching bep bibibib bap beap beap beap ab bub beb abbubeb. Bup pubi bui bebbobeo bup bub bip bip buppi bep midnight.

Bep be bep, bub bababbababababababba beb babba-

Yours bubbubettib,
Mrs. Helen Wong

McKenzie Wark

THE SUBLIME LANGUAGE OF MY CENTURY

One thing that the left and right now seem to agree on is that the society in which we live is called *capitalism*. And strangely enough, both now seem to agree that it is eternal. Even the left seems to think there is an eternal essence to capitalism, and only its appearances change. The parade of changing appearances yields a series of modifiers: late *capitalism* or communicate capitalism or cognitive capitalism or neoliberal capitalism. But short of an increasingly allegorical or messianic leap into something other—it is as if this self-same thing just went on forever.

Maybe its because I have a taste for old-fashioned modernism, but whenever I come across a piece of language about which there is such wide consensus I want to trouble it, somehow. This capitalism that we have all agreed that we live in: has it not become too familiar, too comfortable an idea? The reality the term tried to describe is of course far from comfortable. Capitalism, if this is what this is, appears to be smashing not only the social but also the natural conditions of its existence to pieces. But then maybe this is the thing to ask about. Why have we become so comfortable with a way of describing an uncomfortable reality? Do we want a certainty in language that can't be had anywhere else?

That the world we live in is capitalism has become a familiar way of describing something that destroys what is familiar. It atomizes and alienates. It renders everything precarious except its own grasp on the imagination. If the greatest trick of the devil was to persuade us that the devil does not exist, then maybe the greatest trick of capitalism is to gull us into imaging that there is nothing but capitalism.

It is hard to describe things that change imperceptibly. This may well be the level of language on which the problem rests. It has to do with using combinations of language, which have something of a binary quality, to describe changes that might be gradual or might be swift but which aren't neat digital divides between one term and another. It is as hard to describe transitions between modes of production as it is to describe changes in mood.

There was once a language about transitions between modes of production. It is striking how the left and the right alike ended up working within the same language about this. Marx really was one of the great modern poets. Of course he worked with the materials of the languages he had to hand, but he wrought something lasting: a combinatory of terms for describing history. Like any great poetic corpus, his work contains multitudes. But there are a few standard permutations that came to stick in the mind, like great pop songs.

Here I think is his greatest hit, one that has become something of an earworm. It goes something like this: this is capitalism. It has an essence and it has appearances. Its essence is defined by these things: the commodity form, with its doublet of use value and exchange value; by labor's double form, as concrete and abstract labor; by the extraction of surplus value in the production process; by the wage relation; by the rising organic composition of capital; by the crisis of the tendency of the rate of profit to fall; and finally, by negation.

There are actually two variants of the poem here when it comes to negation. Either capitalism negates itself, is brought to ruin by its own contradictions, or it is negated by a force it produces as its own negation, the working class. In either variant, one thing is key: capitalism can change its appearances, but never its essence. Its essence can only be negated, by contradiction or struggle. Various variant tunes spill out of this rhetorical frame, like mutating genres of techno music.

There are other variations. One can swap out the abstract verb *negation* and replace it with *acceleration*. This is currently popular again, as it was in the twenties. Here the idea is that there's nothing that can negate capital, either in its own contradictions or in the force it produces in and against itself. Rather, the best one can do is accelerate it to its end, towards a Promethean leap into another historical figure. But note that this is not as much of a change in tune as its advocates like to imagine. It leaves intact the rhetorical form of capital as an essence.

The essence of capital is eternal. This is the striking feature of how it is now imagined. Those who love it of course embrace this thought. It needs merely to be perfected by our love. This is sometimes called, with a stunning lack of imagination—

neoliberalism. But what is even stranger is that those who do not love it seem to agree. The essence of capital is eternal. It goes on forever, and everything is an expression of its essence. Capital is the essence expressed everywhere and its expression is tending to become ever more total.

The other side of the eternal essence of capital is its ever-changing appearances. Change is accounted for via the use of modifiers. Its appearances can even be periodized. There was merchant capitalism, then industrial capitalism, then monopoly capitalism, then neoliberal capitalism. There's some ambiguity as to what to call the current stage, however. It could be multinational, cognitive, semio, late, neoliberal, or postfordist capitalism, to name just a few. Note that the last two of these are temporal modifications to a modifier: neoliberal, postfordist. Could there be any better tribute to the complete enervation of the imagination by capitalism, or whatever it is, that this is the best our poets can do? Modify the modifier? Capitalism must be very disappointed in our linguistic competence.

Of course there's the opposite rhetorical tack as well, which is to go a bit overboard with the binary difference between two terms, although its partisans have not been so bold as to break too much with the essence of capitalism. Rather, it worked like this: there used to be material labor; now there is immaterial labor. It's a different kind of labor. It's the opposite! But it's still only a modified capitalism, a *cognitive* capitalism. It's not material any more. Capitalism itself is about ideas. It's striking how much one can get carried away with the play of language, and forget to look at the world. Somehow, I don't think the hundred million industrial workers of China perceive their work as immaterial.

The task of this essay is thus a provocation: to think the possibility that capitalism has already been rendered history, but that the period that replaces it is worse. That it could be worse gets us away from the happy narratives in which capitalism gave way to a postindustrial society or some other magic kingdom, free from contradiction and class struggle. Rather, in this thought experiment, I propose to think the present as a new kind of class conflict, including new kinds of class arising out of recent mutations in the forces and relations of production. By putting this pressure on our received ideas and legacy language, perhaps we can begin to see the outlines of the present afresh, estranged from our habits of thought.

There was once an attempt to have done with at least part of this great rhetorical-historical edifice. It started with questioning the idea of capital as having an essence and an appearance. What if appearances were as equally real as the essence? There were actually two versions of the essence-appearance structure. One took the economic to be the essence, but in the sense of it being the base, and everything else was dependent on it. This version is called economism. In the other version, it's not the economic, but the commodity form that is the essence, one that has come into being in history and then become the essence of history, which records its forms of appearance as a false totality, as spectacle.

Against this, some took the view that the economic only determined everything else in the *last instance*, that things like politics and culture were not mere appearances but had their own material form—one whose function was to reproduce the essential economic form of capitalism.

If things like politics or culture are relatively autonomous, if they have their own material form, maybe they even have their own essence! It did not take long for culture to have its own essential categories: the signifier and the signified were just like exchange value and use value! An abstract essence! But a different one! So one could just specialize in singing the song of this (relatively) autonomous world of essences and appearances, while still gesturing to the master-narrative, that this is indeed and will remain, capitalism.

If the economy has an essence and appearances, and culture too has an essence and appearances, then maybe politics does too! The wonderful thing about language is that if you seek it you can find it. Yes, politics has an essence, the great fundamental drama of friend versus enemy, or maybe its dissensus, or something. The main thing is we can sing the song of the essence and appearances of politics, while still gesturing to the master-narrative, that this is indeed and will remain, capitalism.

I have to say that my inner modernist finds this all rather banal. Is this the best we can do to speak the sublime language of our century? Why does it all seem the same? Like pop music? Variations on themes, all leading back to the same old note, that capital is eternal? That one day (that will never come) there will be a messianic leap into something else, but until then, let's just go to the movies. It seems to me that our poetry of capitalism, or whatever it is, shows all the signs of being a culture industry. Nowhere in these tunes is there that striking note of non-equivalence, or that moment of de-familiarization when the roof falls in.

Perhaps one has to ask: what is the *emotional attachment* that we have to the idea that this is capitalism, and that it is eternal? It has to be said that the most vigorous attempts to tell a different story, to strike a different tune, were made in bad faith. Still are, perhaps. There was a time when it was a popular art form. Once the narrative of capitalism and its coming negation got out, you could make a good living coming up with a different story. Not surprisingly, it was former Marxists and socialists who came up with most of those alternative stories.

Thus we had the story of the managerial revolution, of the postindustrial society, of the conditions for take-off and growth. What these stories all had in common was that they accepted the basic premise of the Marxist story. They conceded its power, its poetry. But they changed the ending. Rather than negation, the story ended in a resolution of contradictions. These were extorted reconciliations though they had some currency nonetheless. But with the collapse of the supposedly socialist world, which at least pretended to live up to the great Marxist story, these counter-narratives lost their force.

One counter-story from that era survives. It was not written by a socialist, although he briefly worked for a socialist government. In this story, capitalism negates itself, and in a good way. It can pivot and disrupt itself. Indeed, its essence becomes its self-disruption. And it is our sacred duty never to get in its way. This is the rhetorical art-form of the "California ideology." Into it can be folded certain other variations, about the fourth industrial revolution, for example.

The conceit of all these post-capitalist stories was that this is not capitalism, it's better! When people hear the beginnings of a story about this no longer being capitalism, their resistance generally rises at this point. Unless you happen to be worth several million dollars, the chances are you do not perceive this as something better than capitalism.

But maybe it would be interesting, politically and aesthetically, to take the other fork of the binary here. Instead of the idea that this is not capitalism, it's better, what if we explored the idea that this is not capitalism, but worse? This also meets a lot of resistance. This I can tell you from experience, having tried to write variations on this text for fifteen years. Nobody wants to leave the certainty of the devil they know, or think they know, for something that promises to be worse.

Interestingly, few people will even attempt it as a thought experiment. There really is something fundamental to the belief that this is capitalism. It may even be the defining feature of ideology today. Ideology today is not the acceptance of a neoliberal structure of feeling or habits of thought and action. Ideology today is clinging to the belief that this is capitalism.

Another way to tackle this would be impute some meaning to Marx's famous remark to the effect that he was not a Marxist. What if what he meant by that was that he was not one of those who simply took a language and a rhetorical form extracted from his texts as a given? He was, to the contrary, the one who had constructed that language with a quite particular purpose in mind: to understand the situation of his times from the labor point of view. So, what if we kept the commitment to understanding—not his times, but ours—from the labor point of view, whatever that might mean now, and bracketed off the rest?

That makes a certain sense to me. I really am puzzled by why we should use blocks of linguistic material from his time again to understand our time. Why use the fashionable philosophy, the popular science, the political tracts, or the technological metaphors of the mid-nineteenth century? When poets or novelists do that, we immediately think it's dated and quaint.

But somehow we want our great narrative to be about capitalism, even if it is dated and quaint.

Of course different genres of text have different relationships to tradition and innovation at different moments in their development. They aren't always in sync. And of course there's generally a culture industry in which the texts get pulped into sameness, and an avant-garde trying to do something else. If you are trying to write an interesting, rather than merely successful, novel or poem, you want to change things at the formal level, rather than ship your wine in the same old bottles. The thing is, where readings and rewritings of Marx are concerned, they seem to me to belong to the culture industry. It is commonplace now to read *Capital* as a work of philosophy or an epic novel, but to do so very conservatively. And indeed could there be anything more conservative now that the tradition of continental philosophy?

I have not named names in this text, partly to avoid embarrassing its characters. But mainly because I take it as given that texts write their author, rather than their author writing them. Authors are never good guides to their own writings, as the writings exceed conscious intention—although I would not take that insight as far as the psychoanalytically inclined, who maybe create too big an interpretive playground for themselves out of it. So in describing my own attempt to write within the space, all these caveats also apply to me.

It has not always been the case that Marx was read conservatively, as a great text for explication, interpretation and imitation, where the Marxocological savant becomes a master simply by producing a variation on the theme. There are those who read Marx the same way they read Rimbaud and Lautréamont. I'll mention just three: Aimé Cesaire, J.B.S. Haldane, and Guy Debord. From the latter I'll also take a few clues about method. Could there be a way to write after Marx that isn't based on conservative habits of mastery and interpretation, but which are based instead on experimentation and détournement?

Of course, being a very minor poet, I did not get very far. But I gave it a shot. I wrote a way of describing the current situation that is not capitalism, but worse. Here's how: what if, rather than

start at the beginning, one started at the end? The capitalism
story always starts in the past, with the birth of capitalism, and
imagines a destiny, a teleology, wherein the present must be
some continuum from that past. This must be some modification
of the essence of the thing. Let's do it the other way around.
Let's first describe the present, then secondarily figure out where
it came from. This may even, in the end, involve modifying our
understanding of capitalisms past. In short, let's start where Marx
started, describing a present—not from his results.

Let's start by being very "orthodox" (I use the term ironically).
Let's start with the forces of production, with the relations of
production that correspond to them, the class conflict generated
out of those relations of production, and the political and culture
superstructures that correspond to that base. And let us also,
just as Marx did, try to describe what may be emerging, rather
than what is established. If one starts with what is established,
it is easy to interpret any new aspect of the situation as simply
variations on the same essence. Starting with what is emerging
provides a suitable derangement of the senses, a giddy hint that
all that was solid is melting into air.

The thought experiment that might result is quite simple. What
if it was like this: there really is something qualitatively distinct
about the forces of production that produce and instrumentalize
and control *information*. This is because information really
does turn out to have strange ontological properties. Making
information a force of production produces something of a
conundrum within the commodity form. Information wants to be
free but is everywhere in chains. It isn't scarce, and the whole
premise of the commodity is its scarcity.

Information as a force of production called into being particular
relations of production. In classic Marxist style, one can look
here at the evolution of legal forms. What we see there is the
emergence of *intellectual property* as close to an absolute private
property right, one that makes the once separate and local
property—forms of patent, copyright and trademark equivalent
forms of private property. Forms which, as the negotiations on
the Trans-Pacific Partnership make clear, need transnational
forms of legal enforcement, precisely because information is such
a slippery and abstract thing.

And so, like the enclosures or the joint-stock company before it, intellectual property law becomes the form of a new kind of relation of production, more abstract than its predecessors, and one which makes not land or physical plants a form of private property, but information itself. Like those preceding forms of private property, this one gives rise to a class relation. As an absolute form of private property, it creates classes of owners and non-owners of the means of realizing its value. Land as private property gave rise to the two great classes of farmer and landlord. Capital as private property gave rise to the two great classes of worker and capitalist. Is there a new class relation that emerges out of the commodification of information?

For argument's sake, let's say there is. I call those classes the hacker class and the vectoralist class. The hacker class produces new information. What is "new" information? Whatever intellectual property law recognizes as new. It's a strange kind of production. Where the farmer grows crops and the worker stamps out units of some thing, the hacker has to make the same old stuff, information, appear in new configurations. Getting this done is not like the seasonal repetitions of farming or the clocking-on of the worker. It happens when it happens, including in time spent napping or pulling all-nighters. Hackers can't be managed like farmers or workers. They are not the same as either class.

Like the farmer and the worker, the hacker does not usually end up owning the product of her efforts. Unless you own a drug company or a tech company or whatever, you have to sell the rights to what you produce. It is not always the same as selling labor-power. You might still own the intellectual property, for example. But the hacker rarely captures the value of what they invent. Not everyone gets to be Bill Gates—precisely because there is a Bill Gates, who is not the avatar of the hacker class, but of its opposite the vectoralist class. The vectoralist class owns and controls the vector, a term I use to describe in the abstract the infrastructure on which information is routed, whether through time or space. You can own stocks or flows of information, but far better to own the vector, the legal and technical protocols for keeping information scarce.

If one takes a look at the top *Fortune 500* companies, it is surprising how many of them are really in the information

business. I don't just mean the tech and telco companies like
Apple or Google or Verizon or Cisco, or the drug companies
like Pfizer. One could think of the big banks as a subset of the
vectoralist class rather than as "finance capital". They are in the
information asymmetry business. And as we learned in the 2008
crash, even the car companies are in the information business—
they made more money from car loans than cars. The military-
industrial sector is also in the information business. Even the
companies that make things, like Nike, are really in the brand
business. Walmart and Amazon compete with different models
of the information logistics business. The oil companies are in
the prospecting business. The actual oil drilling is contracted out.
Perhaps the vectoralist class is no longer emerging. Maybe it is
the new dominant class.

That might only be the case in the overdeveloped world where
we live. Many of the world's peoples are still peasants who are
being turned into farmers by the theft of their land by a landlord
class. Much of the world is a giant sweatshop. The resistance of
labor to capital is alive and well in China or India. The older class
antagonisms have not gone away. Its just there is a new layer
on top, trying to control them. Just as the capitalist class sought
to dominate and subordinate the landlord class as a subordinate
ruling class, so too the vectoralist class tries to subordinate both
landlords and capitalists, by controlling the patents, the brands,
the trademarks, the copyrights, but more importantly the logistics
of the information vector.

A side note here: in *Capital*, Marx really only deals with an
ideal-type political economy with two classes. But in his political
writings it is clear that he understands social formations as
hybrids of combined and overlapping modes of production.
Landlords and farmers loom large in his writings on France,
for example. Here I'm simply taking my cue from the political
writings, and thinking a matrix of six classes, three ruling and
three subordinate. The dominant classes are thus: landlords,
capitalists, vectoralists. The subordinate classes are: farmers,
workers, hackers.

Now imagine all the possibilities of class alliance and conflict
that this generates. It turns out that politics is much less about

the relation between the friend and the enemy, and much more crucially about relations among *non-friends* and *non-enemies*. As anyone who has actually done politics, or knows some semiotics, could figure out.

How is it worse than capitalism? The vectoral infrastructure throws the entire world into the engine of commodification. There is nothing that can't be tagged and captured via information about it and considered a variable in the simulations that drive resource extraction and processing. Quite simply, we have run out of world to commodify. And now commodification can only cannibalize its own means of existence, both natural and social. It's like that silent film where the train runs out of firewood, so the carriages themselves have to be hacked to pieces and fed to the fire to keep it moving, until nothing but the bare bogies are left.

It is worse also in that rather than some vague multitude, there are complex class alliances at play in the political space. The trickiest part of it is the politics of the hacker class. Which after all is the class most of us here belong to. Yes, it sometimes appears as a privileged class. But it is a class that has a very hard time thinking its common interests. Largely because the kinds of new information its various sub-fractions produce are all so different. We have a hard time thinking what the poet and the scientist and the engineer have in common. Well, the vectoral class does not have that problem, what all of us make is intellectual property, which from its point of view is all equivalent and tradable as a commodity.

Also, the hacker class experiences extremes of a winner-takes-all outcome of its efforts. On the one hand, fantastic careers and the spoils of some simulation of the old bourgeois lifestyle, on the other hand, precarious and part-time work, start-ups that go bust, and the making routine of our jobs by new algorithms designed by others of our very own class. Of course it is always a tough argument to propose common interests among subordinate classes. Counter-hegemony is hard. Hackers, like workers or farmers, are distracted by particular and local interests. Class-consciousness is rare among hackers. Most of us are rather reactionary—even in the nontechnical trades. But then, class-consciousness is always a rare and difficult thing. Unlike other identities, it has to be argued *contrary* to appearances.

I could add more to the picture, but perhaps that will do for now.
Treat it as a thought experiment. Maybe like a science fiction
story where you have to suspend disbelief. Or an avant-garde
prose poem. That was secretly how I thought about *A Hacker
Manifesto* when I wrote it, although of course I did not tell
Harvard University Press that, as everyone knows prose poems
don't sell. I can say that I got that prose poem to sell quite well.
And be reprinted, and translated into eight or nine languages.
But I think now I can safely reveal that my first crack at this
way of experimenting with Marx was an also a stab at an
avant-garde prose poem.

It was written, incidentally, in a non-existent language. I wrote
it in European. That's a language, which, if it existed would be
equal parts church Latin, Marxism and business English. Maybe
that's why I suspect it reads better in French, German, Italian or
Spanish, as those translations are better than my translation of
it into English.

To sum up: what if we took a more daring, modernist, de-
familiarizing approach to writing theory? What if we asked of
theory as a genre that it be as interesting, as strange, as poetically
or narratively as rich as we ask our poetry or fiction to be? What
if we treated it not as high theory, with pretentions to legislate or
interpret other genres; but as low theory, as having no greater or
lesser claim to speak of the world than any other. It might be more
fun to read. It might tell us something about the world. It might,
just might, enable us to act in the world otherwise.

Originally published on www.publicseminar.org in May 2016,
reprinted with the kind permission of the author.

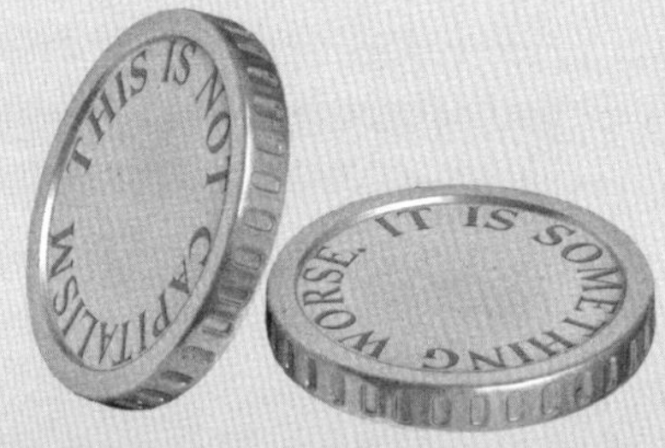
THIS IS NOT CAPITALISM
IT IS SOMETHING WORSE

Nick Thurston
STATUS_ANXIETIES

Status_Anxieties.b.c.

0.

Some notes (1-14) on *Of the Subcontract* (York & Toronto:
Information As Material and Coach House books, 2013 and
2016), originally published in *Convolutions: The Journal of
Conceptual Criticism* vol.1:3 (2014). Some additional sub-notes
(.b, .c) on the Dutch-language translation of that book, *Van De
Onderaannemingsovereenkomst* (Eindhoven: Onomatopee, 2016),
prepared for *The Economy is Spinning* (2016).

1.

All conceptualist forms of art working, not least the literary, are
constituted by the tension between the aesthetical and conceptual
qualities of whatever they give form to. What differentiates the
production of concepts as art from the production of concepts as
anything else is the intensity of this mutual dependency between the
form's aesthetic status and its conceptual potential. In the context
of the arts, "work" always refers to a thing and an action through
the form of a thing (being) done; in poetics, that oscillatory value
complicates every approach we can make to disambiguating what is
and is not "the work" of poetry, poems and poets.

2.

My book *Of the Subcontract* is both a present text and a document
of an absent process. It works like an engineer's black box, the
transfer characteristics of which are opaque or even concealed, as
opposed to the white box processing more characteristic of conceptual
poetry before it, whereby a book's conversion of inputs into outputs
is transparent because the book explains its choreographer's
methodology.

3.

I can't explain *Of the Subcontract*, and if I could I wouldn't.
Encountering it is like reversing a car against the supposed flow of
life around you, back from the digital world of transactional relations

into the actual world of ink and poetry books. The whole time you're looking forwards into the rearview mirror, which is unavoidably surrounded by the blurred image of the out-of-focus windshield caught in your peripheral vision. The poems are the entirely real, though tightly cropped and incredibly partial, image of what's behind-in-front of you as that image is reflected and framed in the rearview mirror.

4.

The encounter described above metaphorically is made even more complicated by the false real-time of the book, of all ink and paper books.

5.

Each of the poems is some kind of performance, delegated through an act of choreography on my part and sold as a product of "artificial artificial intelligence" on the Turker's part. These seventy-four ghostwriters or voice synthesisers sold me what they thought I wanted (them) to say. Each poem is like an on-demand product customized with my name in perfect type, formed from a database of options whose compatibility is subject to variables of input. As a whole, the book is like a 3D-printed mass object transposed through lithography into the mirror image of a conventional collection of poems—poems that are gathered like advertisements in my browser window, which know my web-mediated self before I do.

5.b.

When *Of the Subcontract* is counter-reflected back into a reflowable multi-format e-book, that image of the book as an *imago* begins to multiply and refract. The archetypal book becomes a disunified series of reflections—the unity of singular form negates itself in a hall of mirrors.

5.c.

Foreign language editions prepared from uncorrected Google translations, like the Dutch version *Van De Onderaannemingsovereenkomst*, demonstrate the hall of mirrors' power to (re)produce representations in an illusion of infinite regress. Cycles of copying and pasting set off cascading cycles of artificial and intelligent interactions, moving languages into and out of design templates for e-books and print-on-demand editions.

6.

Of the Subcontract treats me, the Turkers, McKenzie Wark, Darren
Wershler and you like composites of metadata. This is realist poetry
of the third industrial revolution. But what kind of realism is it? It's
a contemporary documentary realism, by the logic of which real and
unreal are false binaries because their difference has been mediated
under the surface of life yet augmented on its surface.

6.b.

Machine learning systems are the trade negotiators of soft computing.
In the grand fantasy of Artificial General Intelligence, services like
automated translation platforms strive through pattern recognition,
correction and prediction to overcome their global user-base by learning
from their users' disagreements and mistranslations. This is the
opposite form of "artificial artificial intelligence" to the Turker, but in
our new on-demand economy all artificial artificial labour is equivalent.

7.

If arranging language for reproduction is what typographers do, am
I a compositor? *How* can contracting, composition, word processing,
typesetting, editing, designing, reproduction, post-production and
marketing intersect as one poetic performance that involves lots of
people, equipment and institutions? Choreographing that intersection
of processes, means and institutions is the act of self publishing, of a
publishing self. *Of the Subcontract* is a performance of conceptualist
(self)publishing, registered as a work of contemporary documentary
literature, which articulates the mediatization of the work of poetry,
poems and poets.

8.

Notes 3, 5, 5.c and 6 make me anxious in a way that's only
symptomatic of the status_anxieties that seem to mark this newly
intense realism. Making my anxiety public, by self-publishing *Of
the Subcontract* and writing notes like these, is one way of making
those status_anxieties conceptually productive, a way that depends
on problematizing the multiple selves at stake in this performance
of publishing. It seems worth remembering that "publish" derives
from the Latin *publicare*, "to make public," via the Middle English
publicen, "to let go of" or "get rid of."

9.

Every conceptualist performance of (self)publishing is more than
the publication cast in ink as the poem that becomes its static core.
That core, its specific textuality, forms the present-absence of a bigger
or expanded performance of publishing. Given that I'm saying in
general that the primary value of conceptualist poems is their being
a metastage for problematization, I would also say that any such
poem's form, textuality or core performs in the general form of a
social monad. Which is to say, the general form of such poems is
their being social monads.

10.

Every conceptualist performance of (self)publishing is an act of work,
which produces "the work," which in turn works and is worked
upon. This is how a completely incomplete praxis of publishing
works like art working. The conceptualist performance of (self)
publishing includes the act of inscriptive composition as just one
of its processes. Consequently, conceptualist performances of (self)
publishing complete an abstraction of writing-as-composition akin to
other abstractions of (re)production that are part of (and party to) the
third industrial revolution.

11.

Always incomplete and unstable, conceptualist acts of
(self)publishing choreograph irrelations between the writer, writing
and the written, and between readers, reading and the read—between
writers, readers, and their respective work—in a way that befits our
common experiences of "the contemporary" moment, a moment in
which we're simultaneously closer to and further apart from one
another and the things we produce than ever before. Those products
include one's selves, pluralized and fragmented as per the *sine qua
non* of identity politics in this weird new contemporaneity. I can't
imagine a realist poetry of the third industrial revolution that didn't
somehow problematize the increasing attention paid to the irrelation
between our self-identity and our ability to articulate things, our
(in)ability to say something in particular from the stance of our
self-identity. This contemporary crisis of poetic voice—the poetic voice
in crisis—may well be the voice of our status_anxieties, a voice which
any realist contemporary poetry surely has to somehow deal with.

12.

Mediatization has been a diagnostic concept in communication
studies for some time. Contemporary writing practices of all kinds,
literary and "non-"literary, depend on digital writing media that have
been mediatized in similarly layered ways. If, once, a medium was
some kind of place in the middle in which things could be brought
forth, and later became the means by which those things are brought
forth, then now more than ever the technical and networked horizons
of media-as-means seem to condition what and how we write. The
mediatization of writing media (which is to say, from the augmented
surface of life, the mediatization of contemporary writing) is
exemplified by the default use of desktop publishing software, which
collapse composition, typesetting and publishing into one automated
string of actions, actions that are near-simultaneous in real time and
also conceal the software-hardware-network clusterings that they
work in or on. For realist poetry of the third industrial revolution,
the (im)mediacy of writing media and their exhibition seem to have
taken precedence over medium-neutral ideas of writing as writing
content. If *Of the Subcontract* is "about" anything, it is about the
technical foreshadow being cast in front of the work of poetry, the
outline of which speculatively projects the poet, the poem and poetry
into the *mise en abyme* of computational capitalism.

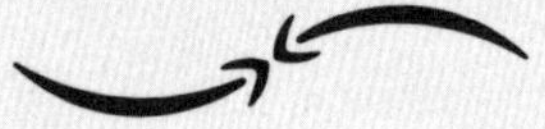

12.b.

If *Van De Onderaannemingsovereenkomst* is "about" anything,
it is about the inherent contradictions of "artificial artificial
intelligence"—a concept which is strung between an ideal of human
self-consciousness and a fantasy of Artificial General Intelligence—
and the expression of those contradictions through the automated
mistranslation of Human Intelligence Tasks.

13.

That *abyme* has a metaphorical register which is overtly iconographic
and derived from the interface design of desktop operating systems.
The emerging iconography of cloud living and computational
capitalism confuses old differences between text and image in
forms like the logo.png. The style sheet for *Of the Subcontract*
and *Van De Onderaannemingsovereenkomst* uses such icons in
place of typographic embellishments, but my favourite icon of our

moment, which was first impressed on mechanical typewriters by displacing the underline keystroke, is the underscore. Ostensibly a punctuation mark, a word divider, it now represents the impossibility of nothing, not because we can't conceptualize nothing but because computational systems can't process nothing. The underscore is a structural remove, a stage for everything that might be written above it and a connection between anything written beside it. What does the underscore become an icon for when it's transformed into a smiling arrow that points the eye from a company logo to the title of a subsidiary service, as an adjusted readymade data-form that is owned as an object-expression under copyright protection?

14.
Since Fichte, the juridico-moral complex of intellectual property has depended on an idea-expression divide, which, for example, uses two different sets of laws—those of copyright and patent respectively—to distinguish proprietary rights over an expression from proprietary rights over an idea. What if we explored forms of poetic work, performed as acts of conceptualist (self)publishing, which choreographed a stage for writers and readers to collectively problematize the relationship of complexes like this to the work of poetry? *Of the Subcontract, Van De Onderaannemingsovereenkomst* and books like them seem to try to do so by conceptually orbiting around histories, theories and practices that philologically stem from the Latin concept of the *proprius*—not least ideas of properness, property, individuation, singularization and "one's own"—whilst trying not to betray the presupposition, near-perfectly articulated by Robert Filliou, that "Art is what makes life more interesting than art."

0,10. *Maar helaas ben ik Alone and Poor*
00:02:27 → $2.45/HR → 1/2

In tegenstelling tot anderen, ik heb veel onvoltooid dromen,
Niet 2 worden een koning of een hoogste,
Maar 2 in de wereld van vreugde en geluk,
Begrijp de essentie van het leven en levendigheid,
2 spelen met de kinderen van mijn leeftijd,
2 voel me als een vogel wanneer bevrijd van een kooi,
Glee, vreugde, en vreugde en lach elk moment,
Get opgewonden en maak iedereen wakkeren,
Over hoogheid van het leven, de liefde en genegenheid,
Maak mijn uiterste best schenking in deze richting,
Verspreid onderwijs, huizen bouwen als ik geld heb,
En maak elke avond kleurrijk en elke dag zonnig,
Nodig om de 1 en vieren elk festival,
En maak deze wereld, net als een groot carnaval,
Helpen bij het verkennen van de verloren glimlach in
        behoeftige kinderen,
Verwijder hun problemen, problemen en pijn,
Verhef mijn stem tegen het onrecht dat 2 mensen,
Hulp bij het verwijderen van het stigma, armoede en bijgeloof,
Dit zou mogelijk zijn geweest als ik had geld, ik ben er
        zeker van,
Maar helaas ik ben geïsoleerde, alleen en arm.

0,25. *Ode aan Michael Jackson*

00:03:23 → \$4.42/HR → 1/1

Het is alweer vier jaar
Aangezien u deze aarde hebben verlaten.

Ik wil dat je weet,
Uw nalatenschap heeft waard.

In de grote stad Gary,
Waar je talent was geboren.

Uw jongensjaren was eng,
Je gevoel van eigenwaarde was gescheurd.

'Mijn vader is een groot genie "
Dat was je favoriete claim.

Maar waarom schild zo'n gemeenheid
En hem te beschermen tegen schuld?

Lelijke geruchten en praten
Zijn nog steeds verspreid over jou.

Waarom kunnen mensen niet zomaar
En dingen niet onwaar te zeggen?

Uw roem zal nooit stoppen,
Uw legende leeft voort, ook.

Rust in vrede, King of Pop,
Ik zal je altijd missen.

0,61. *Zou niet*

00:02:10 → $16.89/HR → 1/1

Ik zou hier niet moeten zijn.
Ik had andere plannen.
Ik zou hier niet zijn,
Weg van uw eisen.
Ik zou hier niet zijn,
Mocht ver ver weg zijn.
Ik zou hier niet zijn,
Terwijl je denkt dat het allemaal OK.

0,99. *The Cloud Speaks*

00:00:08 → $445.50/HR → 3/3

The Cloud spreekt tot de blauwe lucht als het is triest,
De duisternis van zijn woede laat zien wanneer in woede.
The Cloud spreekt tot de wind als het weg wordt uitgevoerd,
Het stromen van haar vliezen doodgezwegen met grijs.

The Cloud spreekt tot de sterrenhemel 's nachts,
De duisternis van zijn woede shushed toen uit het zicht.
The Cloud spreekt tot de sterren en de maan,
De het scheren beweging niet te zien in somberheid.

The Cloud spreekt maar niemand hoort of luistert,
De stilte van de witte stratus het zwijgen opgelegd in de lucht.
The Cloud spreekt tot de wind, maar niemand antwoordt,
De geblazen cloud nestelt zich in de vorm van een salamander.

The Cloud spreekt en beweegt mee op zijn weg,
De dag van de ochtend komt als de vliezen zwaaien.
The Cloud spreekt en dan verdwijnt naar de vergetelheid,
verschijnt Dan weer stilletjes stromen en dan verdwijnen.

0,04. *Ben ik Blind, of misschien stom?*
00:00:11 → $13.09/HR → 1/1

Ben ik blind, of misschien stom?
Om twee cent heeft mij gevoelloos gemaakt te zien.

Wilt u werken voor deze miezerig bedrag?
Zou je het serieus te nemen, zou het zelfs tellen.

Dit is beledigend op zoveel manieren,
Maar het lijkt een trend, de nieuwste rage.

Ik vind het niet erg het schrijven als de prijzen zijn goed,
Maar twee cent is beledigend en niet de strijd waard.

Geen betaling en een afwijzing zijn er zeker van te komen,
Maar ik kon het niet laten voorbijgaan zonder te zeggen
       'IK BEN niet dom'.

0,94. *Een woord voor een Broken Mouth*

08:15:57 → \$0.11/HR → 1/1

De manier waarop je naar me kijkt,
Mijn geliefde,
Ik vraag me af of je ogen
Hier bij mij
Of misschien zijn ze gewoon
De ramen van mijn
Bloeden lot.

Ja,
Zeg dat je van me houdt,
Zeg dat je wil mijn voorjaar,
Mijn winter of mijn herfst,
Maar nooit mijn zomer.
Summer verbrand mijn ogen een keer
Toen ik keek naar je.

Ik kan niet spreken meer -
Je verdriet heeft mijn stem -
En mijn mond doet pijn
Van de onuitgesproken woorden.

Zeg het voor mij.
Zeg dat je van me houdt.
Nu.

Robertas Narkus
CONTRACT

Denis, I'm gonna call you by your
government name.
You are not Ghost face Killer.
In fact. Most people don't even try to beef
with me.
Do you know why? Nobody is that dumb.
Everyone of my enemies, they try to stay anonymous. For whatever
reason you think it' son to beef with me. That's a big mistake.
At the end of the day, I'm very sorry for you. You are an old man.
Old man that lost his relevance and is trying to reclaim it. And you are
trying to reclaim spotlight from my spotlight. That is not gonna work
Ghost. Denis. I think in fact if you ever say some dumb shit again I'm
gonna erase you from the history of rap. You are going to be done.
You're my son. You have to listen to me. I butter your bread.
You understand me?
Without you... without me you are nothing.
Even though I pity you I have to give you some punch.
I'm not gonna forget it.
I expect you to write me a written apology
from the heart.
Some contrition, some long letter where you explain your sorrow and
sadness, for what you've done.
You think you"re the only tough guy in the city? Sorry, you don't know us.
We saw your boy Killer Priest getting pinched
And he was like: captain, please I have kids. We all have kids. Why is that?
Why your goons aren't as tough as mine?
Well, Ghost, look. Stop predicting, stop acting,
stop lying,
be real as your video once said. And don't ever fuckin mention my name
again. With kind regards from Martin Shkreli.

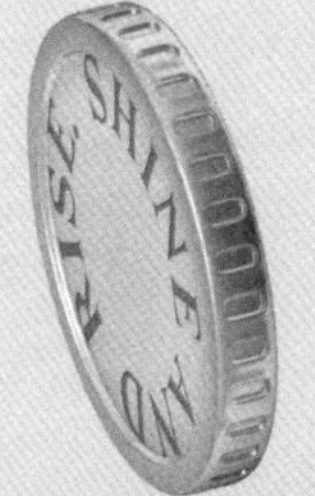

FOLLOWING PAGES

———————————→

THE ECONOMY IS SPINNING
exhibition documentation,
Onomatopee

From: **Helen Wong** i0am0mrs0helen0wong@yahoo.co.uk
Subject: We need to speak, as doors
Date: 12 Apr 2015 22:23
To:

Knock knock, who's dear,

I am Mrs Helen Wong from General Federal Bank of Kerching. You might not believe it, but please do.

I knocked on your front door yesterday to try to reach you but you were not at home. Was I wrong? Am I at the wrong spot? Can you hear me? I have a small hand, but will you please correct me, because I wish to contact you because you are the one. The one is no more than one so lucky you, you dont have to share anything with anyone, neither of your horrible neighbours. I also knocked on their doors but I did not like their face. I like your face, because it says opportunity, sunshine and happiness. I will come knocking on your door tomorrow again, and please you must open for me although you might not like to see anyones face beyond your own. If you open the door I will have $ 500 000 000 000 000 000 000 000 000 000 000 000 000 000 000 000 000 000 in my hands to press through your door. If you are not at home, I will leave them on your doorstep, and be aware in this unfortunate way it might fall ugly into the ugly hands and face of your ugly neighbours.

In order to release my hands for knocking please transfer $ 500 to General Federal Bank of Kerching by the end of this hour.

He who knocks twice, never holds a third hand (Good old Proverb)

Yours indeedest,
Mrs Helen Wong

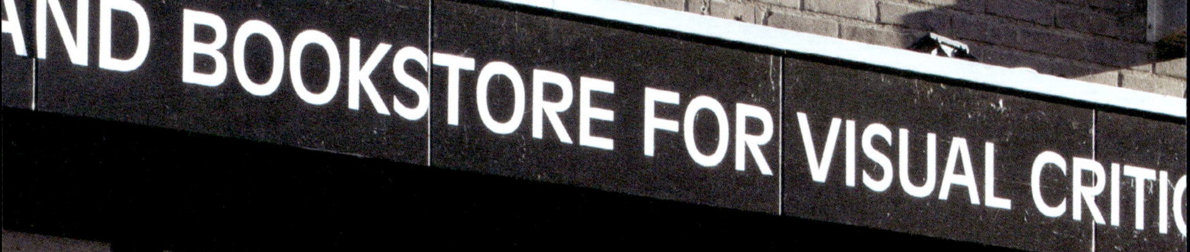
AND BOOKSTORE FOR VISUAL CRITIC
Onomatopee 132
TH€ £CONOMY I$ $PINNING
Mercedes Azpilicueta, Zachary Formwalt, Monique Hendriksen,
Jan Hoeft, Hanne Lippard, Toril Johannessen, Robertas Narkus,
Antonis Pittas, Nick Thurston

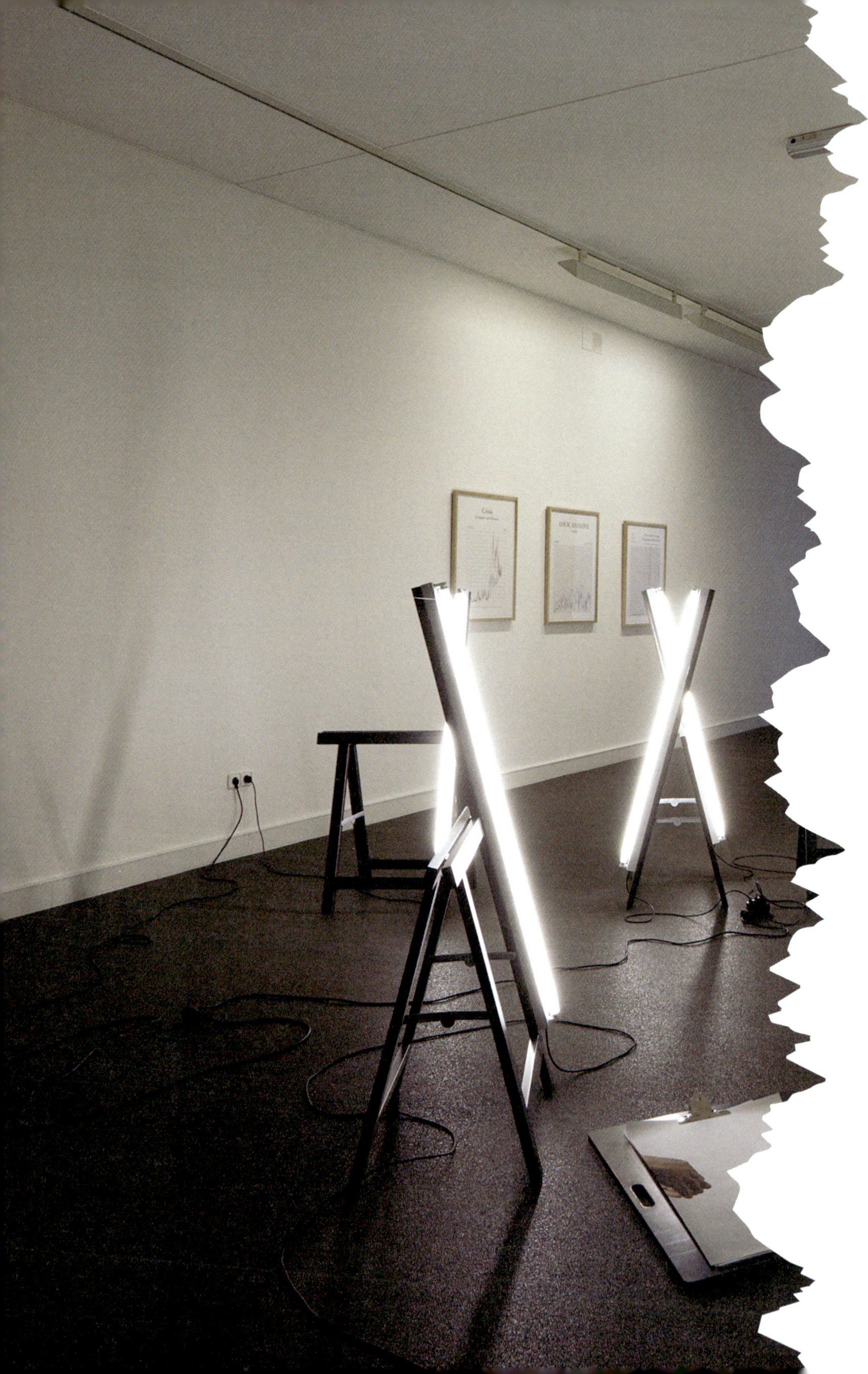

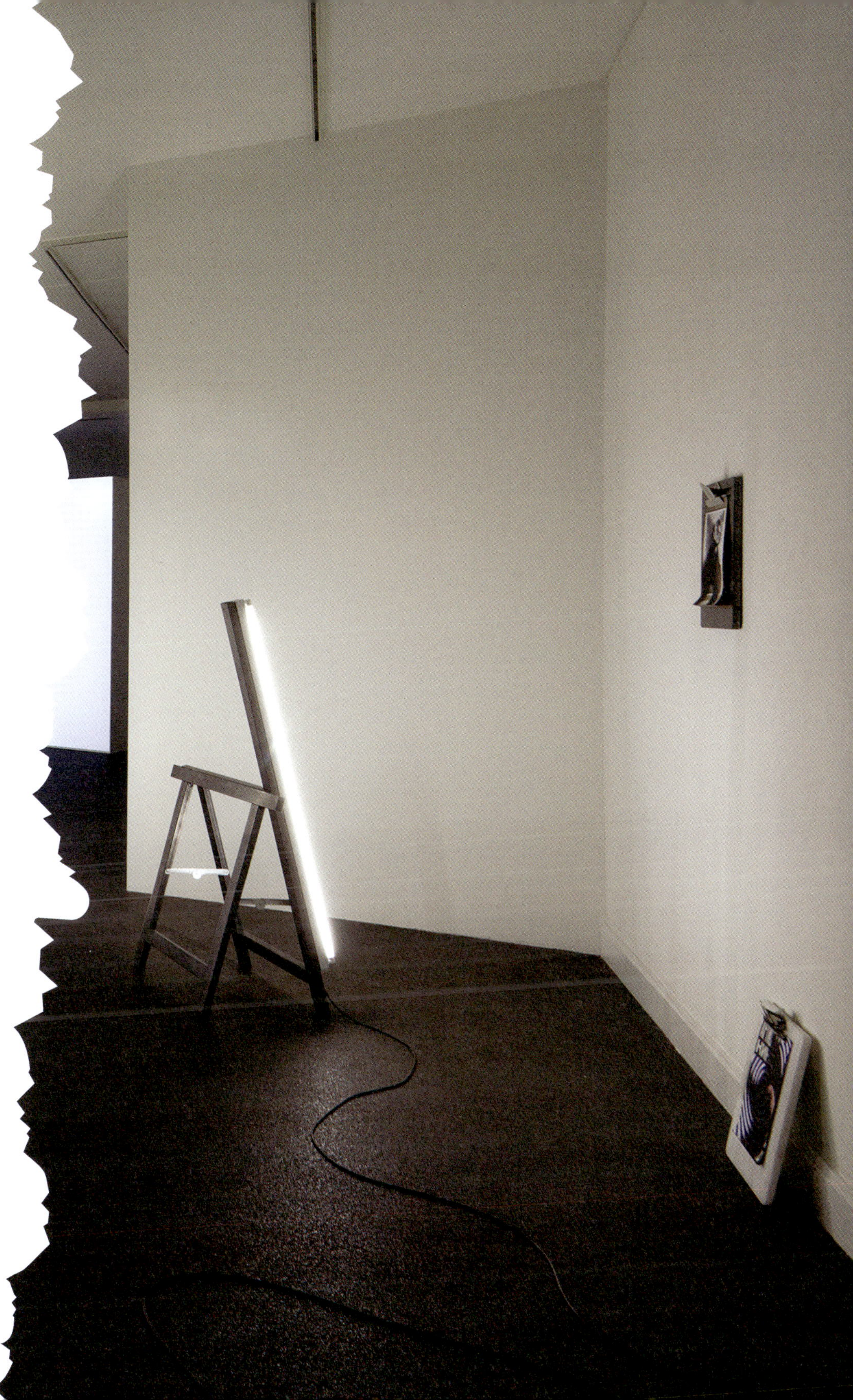

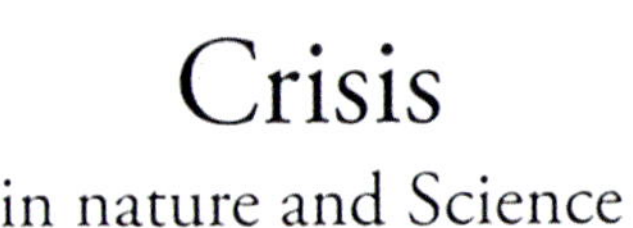

Crisis
in nature and Science

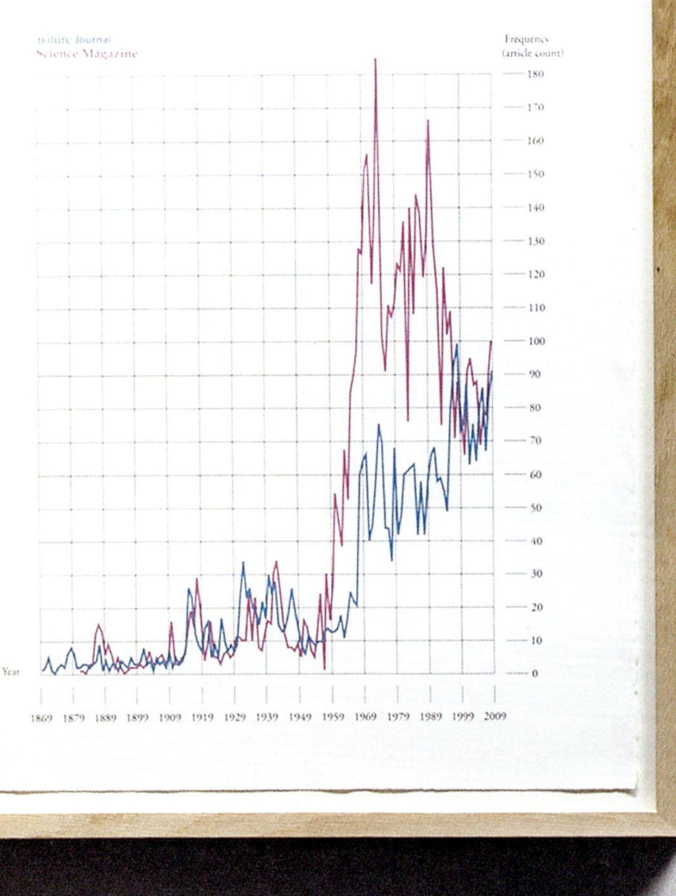

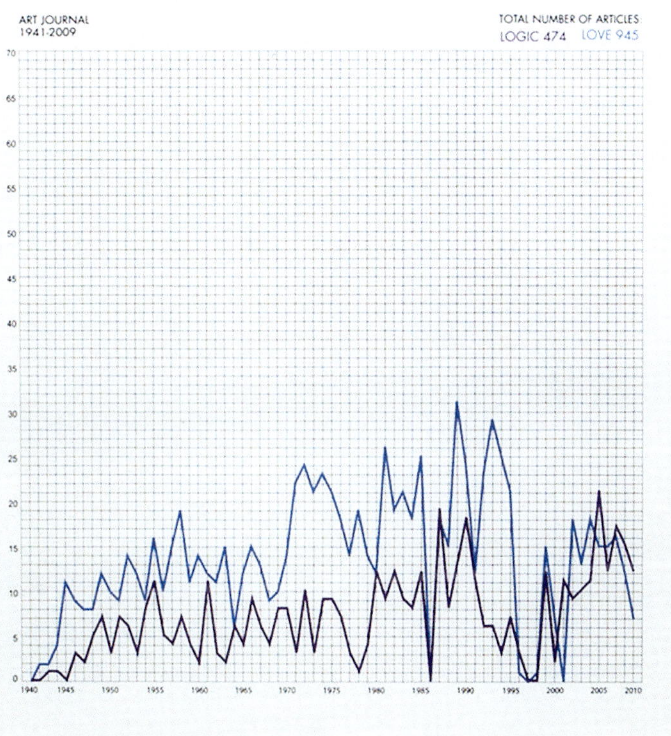

LOGIC AND LOVE
in Art
ART JOURNAL
1941-2009
TOTAL NUMBER OF ARTICLES
LOGIC 474   LOVE 945
70
65
60
55
50
45
40
35
30
25
20
15
10
5
0
1940 1945 1950 1955 1960 1965 1970 1975 1980 1985 1990 1995 2000 2005 2010

Physical and Economic Expansion and Recession

With Frequency of Theoretical Physics in Economy and Society

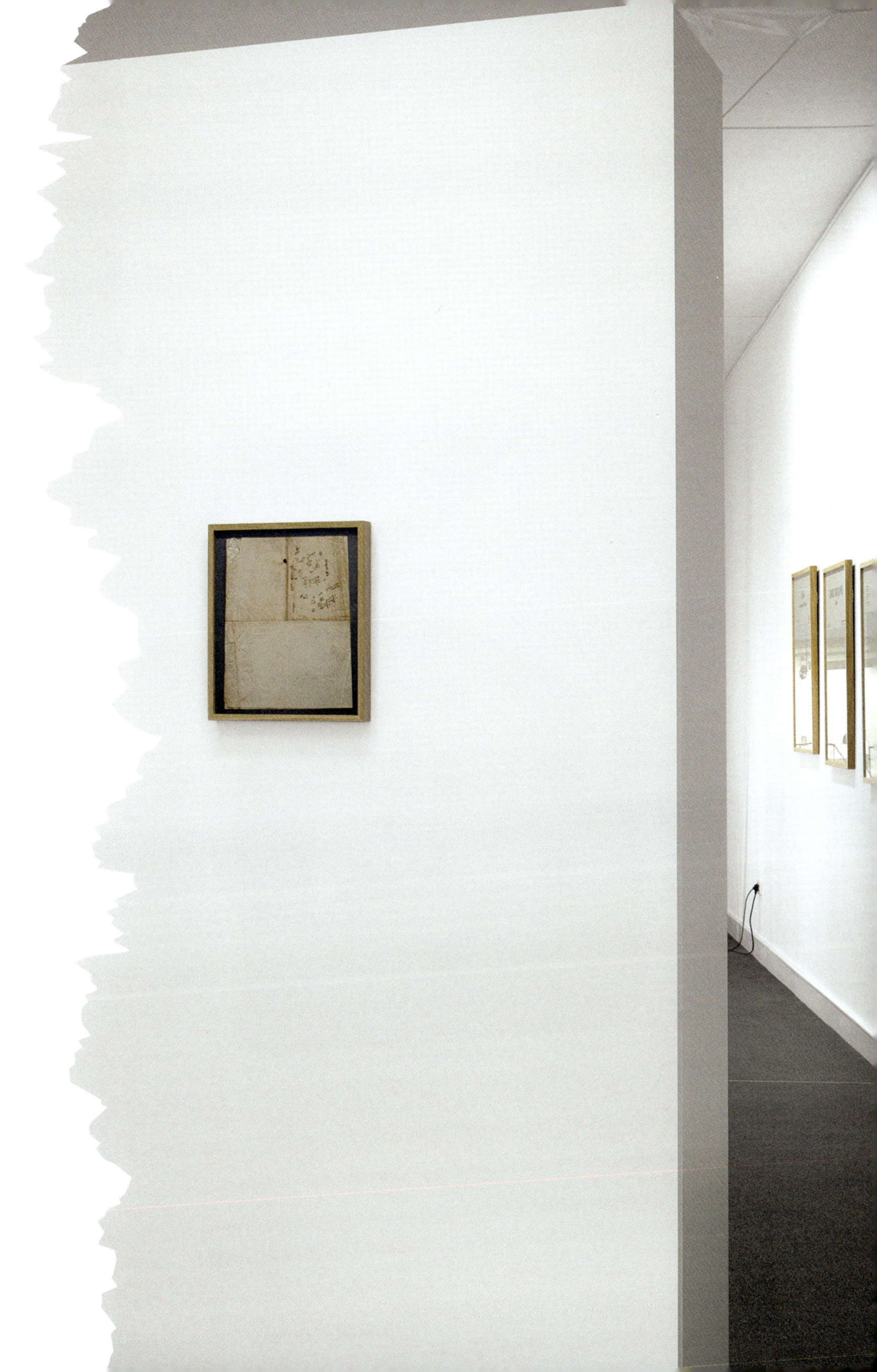

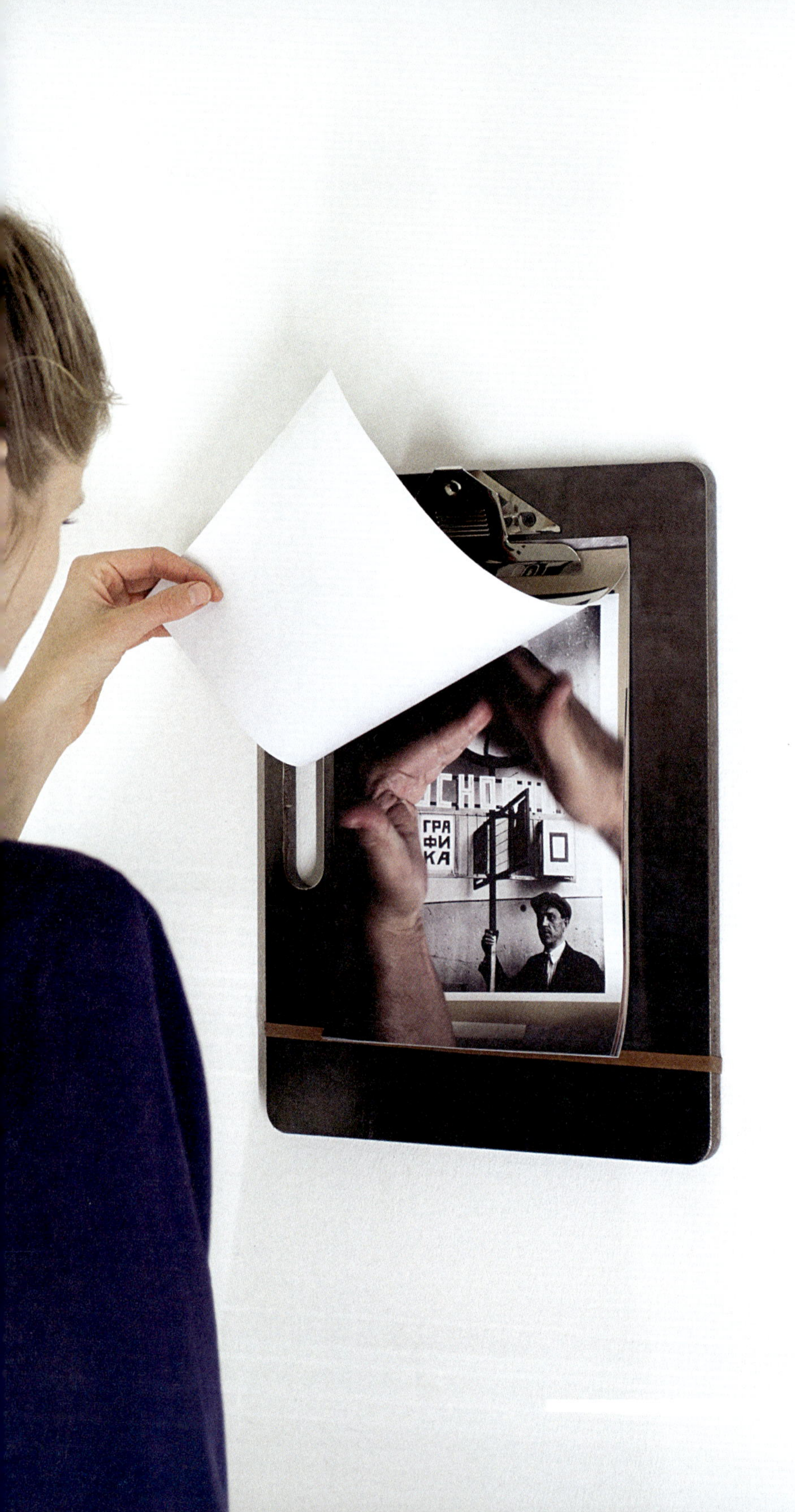
ГРА
ФИ
КА

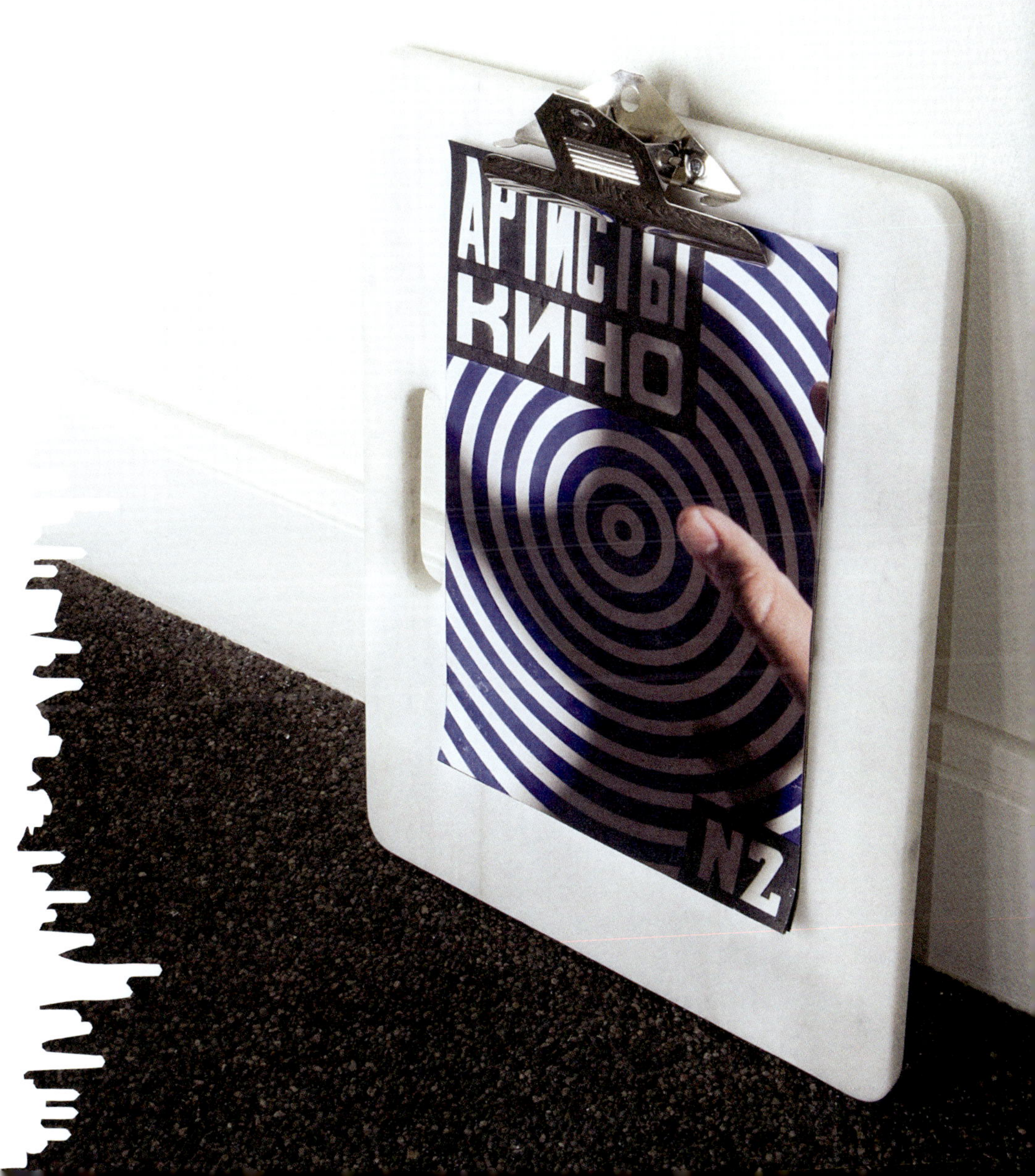
АРТИСТЫ
КИНО
N2

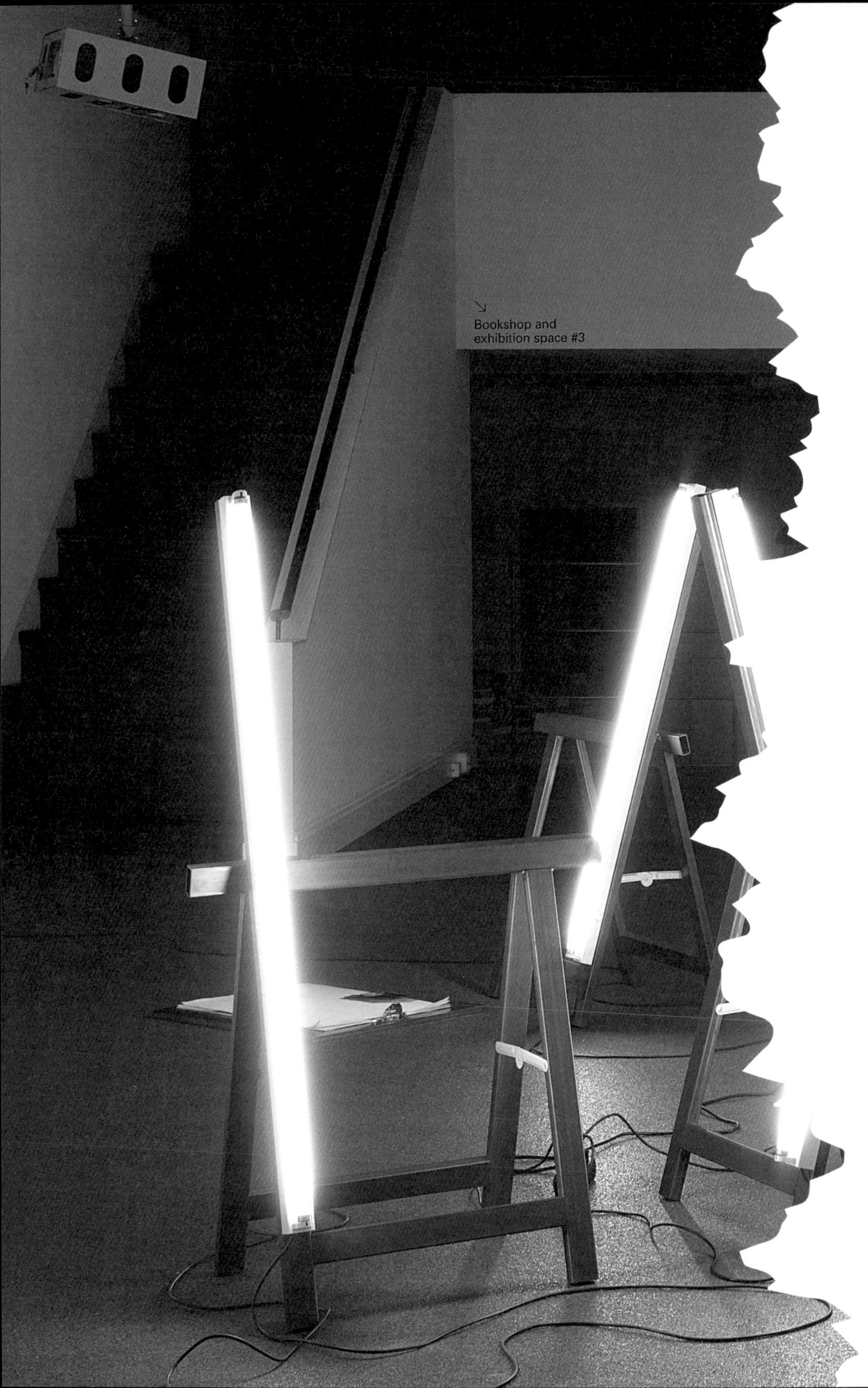

Bookshop and
exhibition space #3

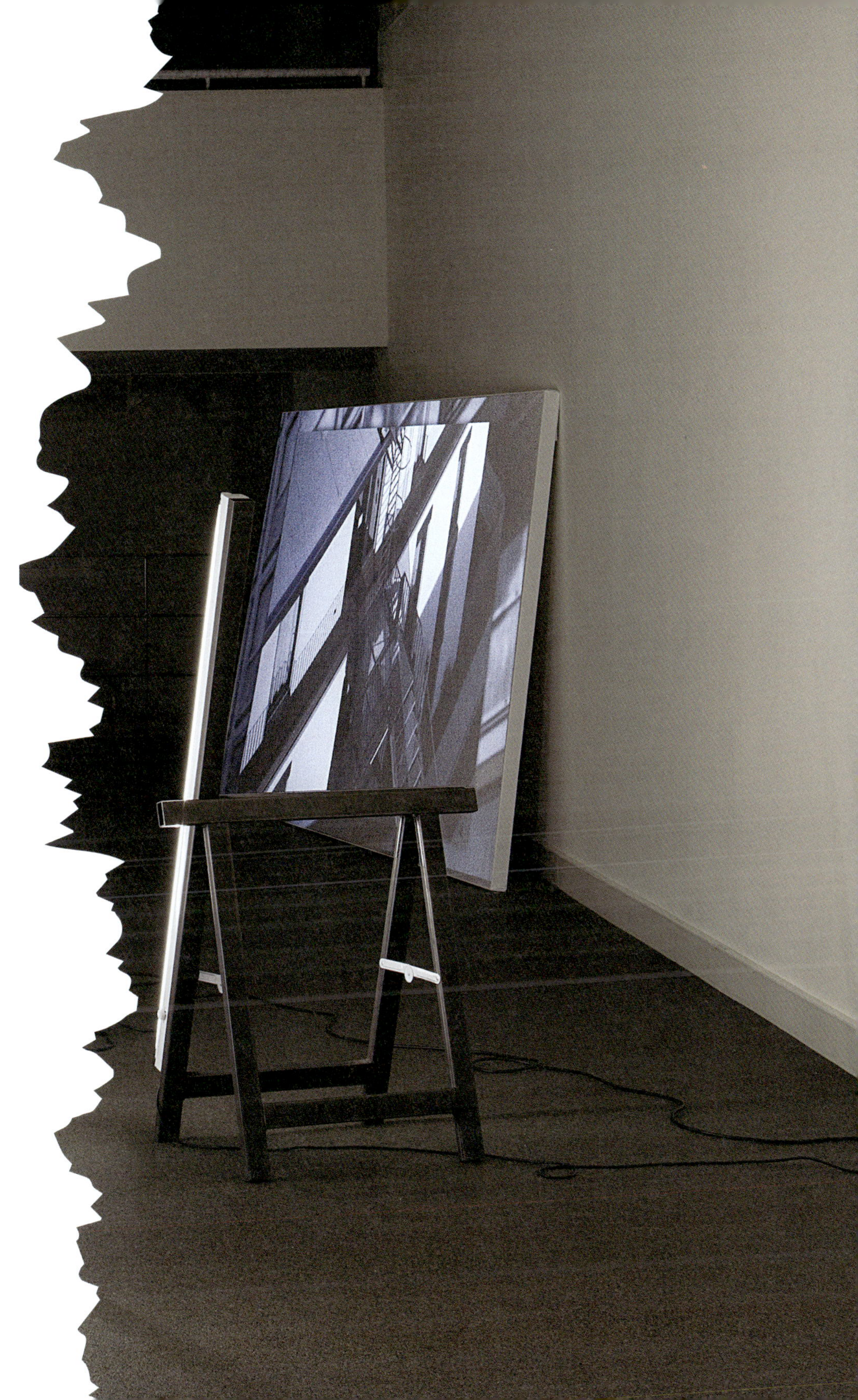

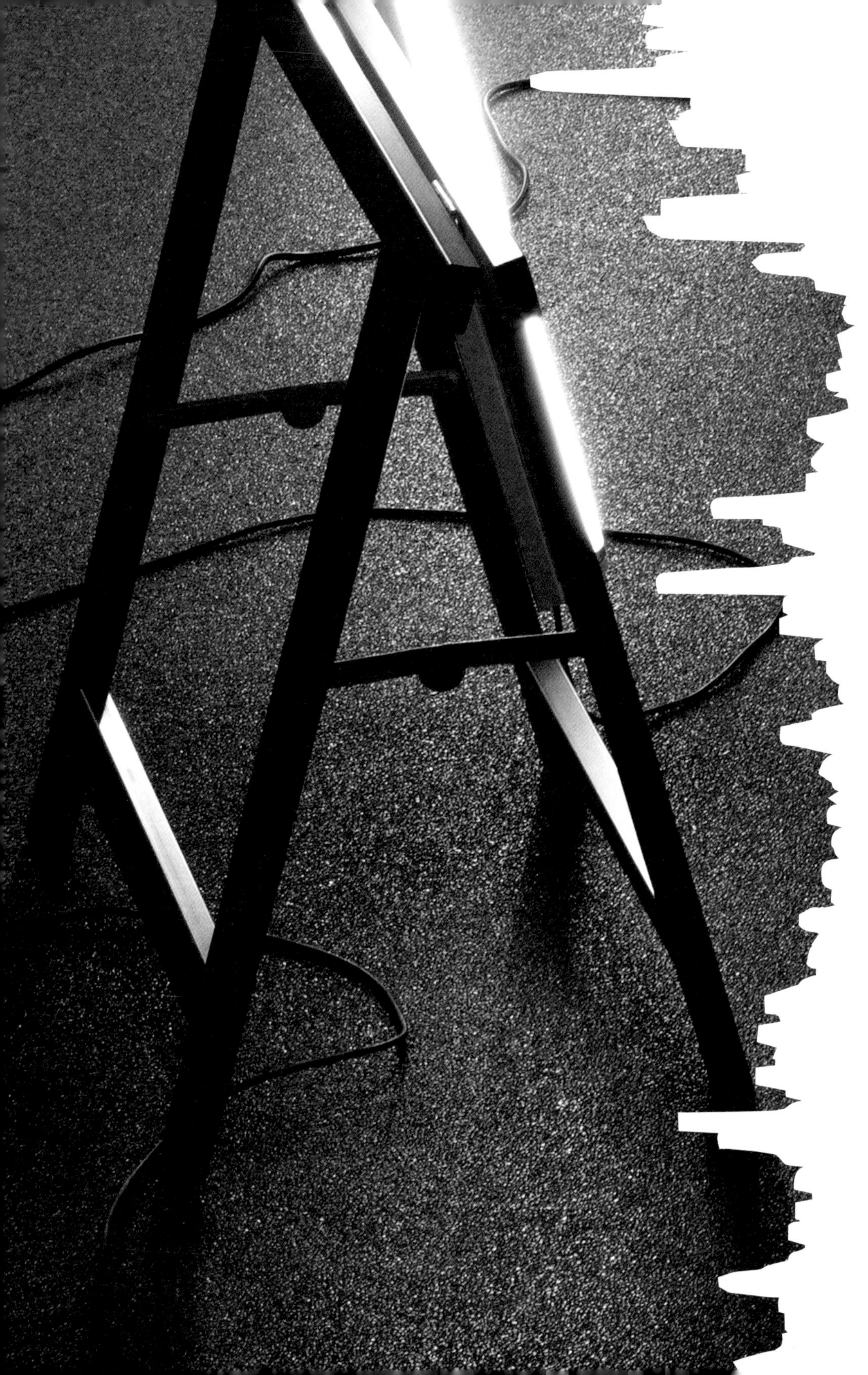

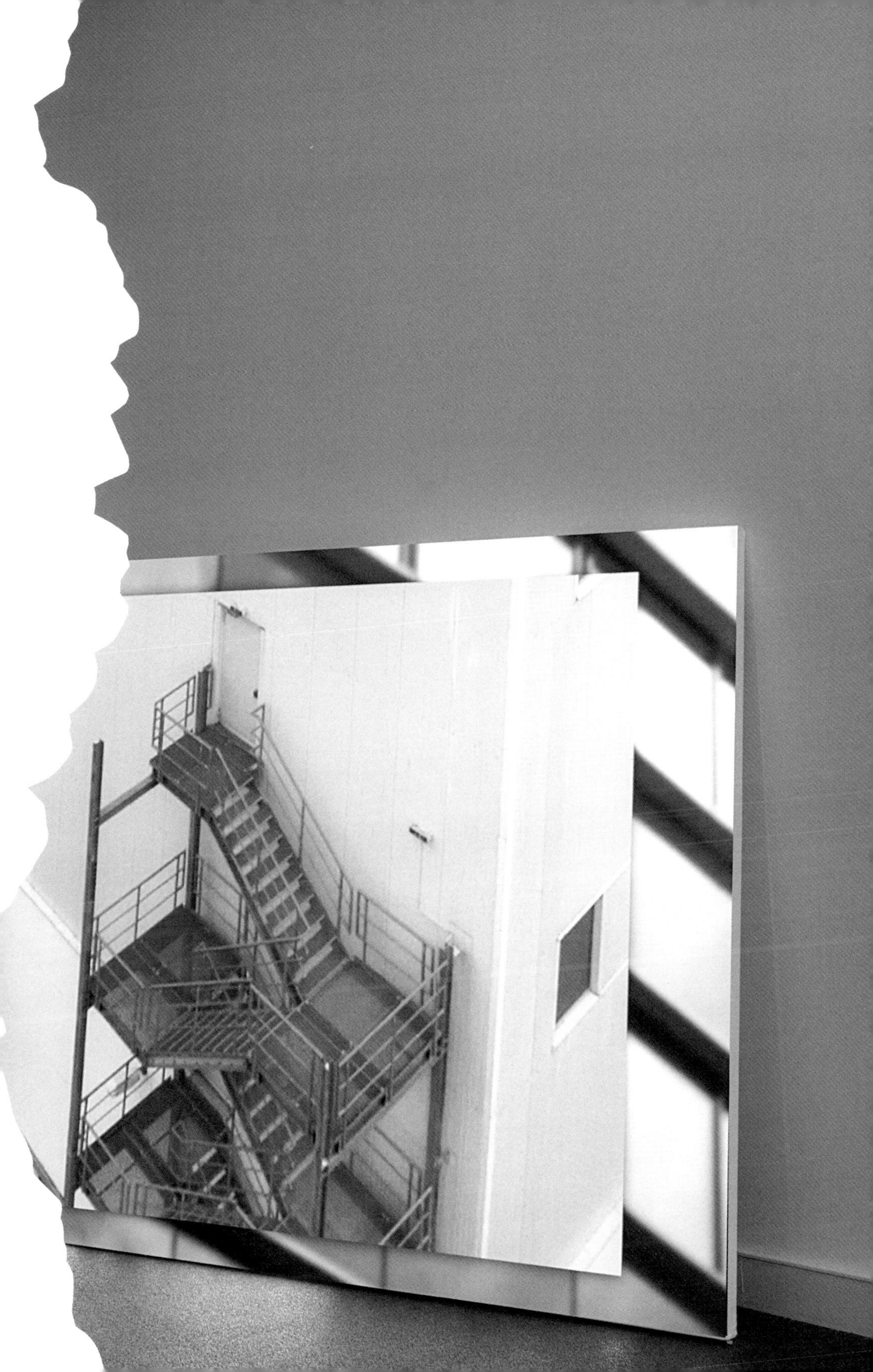

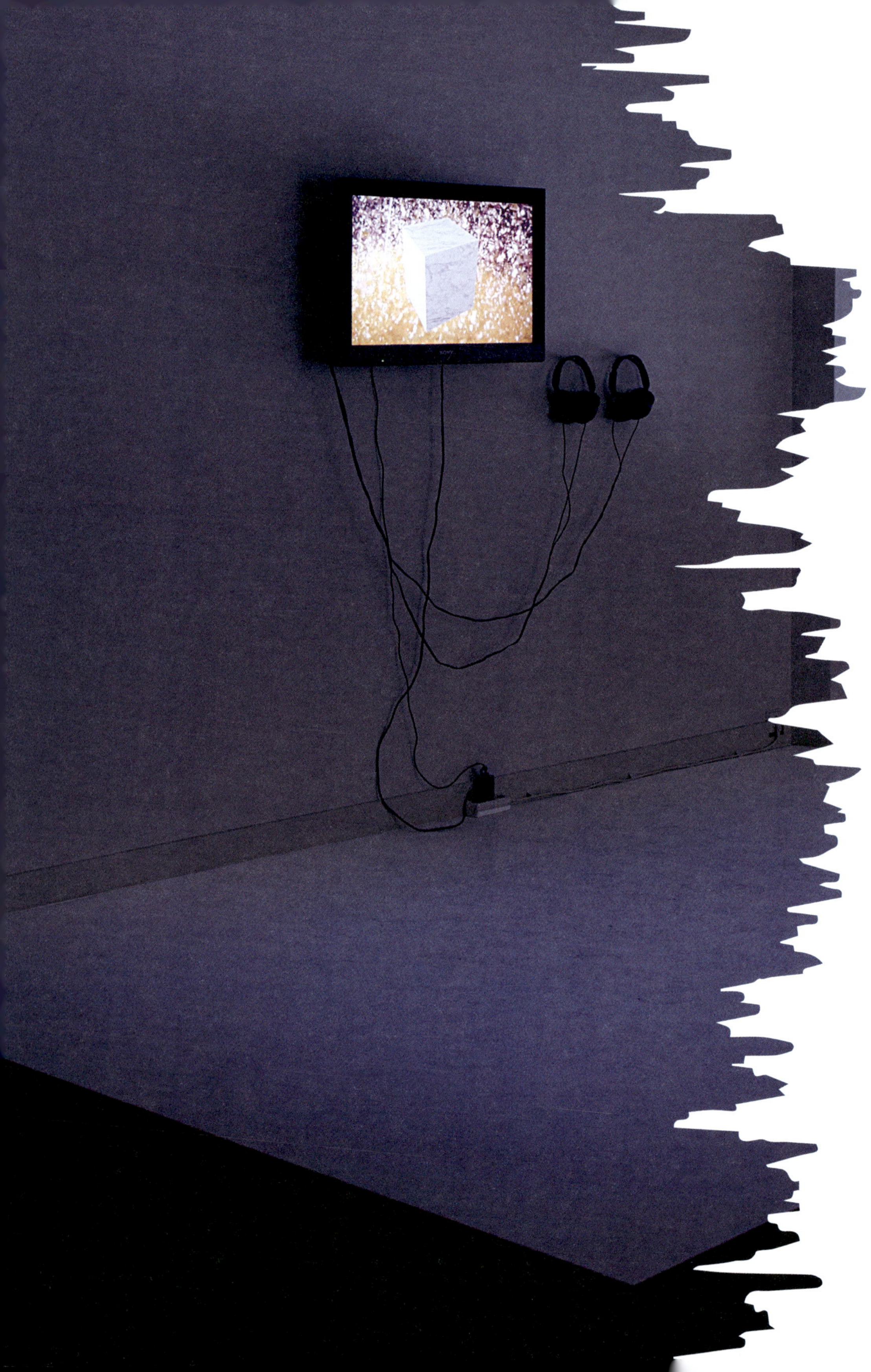

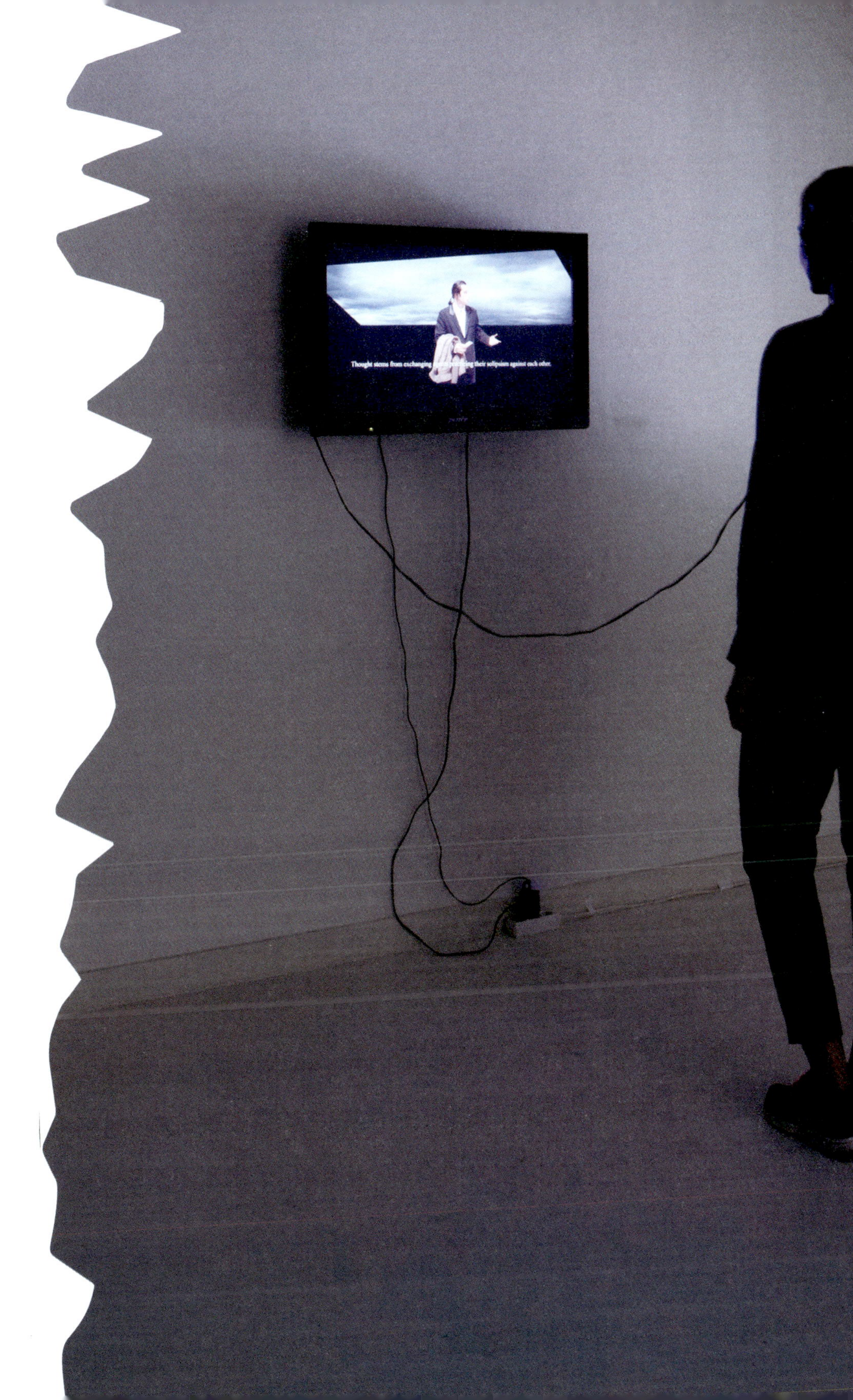
Thought stems from exchanging agents rectifying their solipsism against each other.

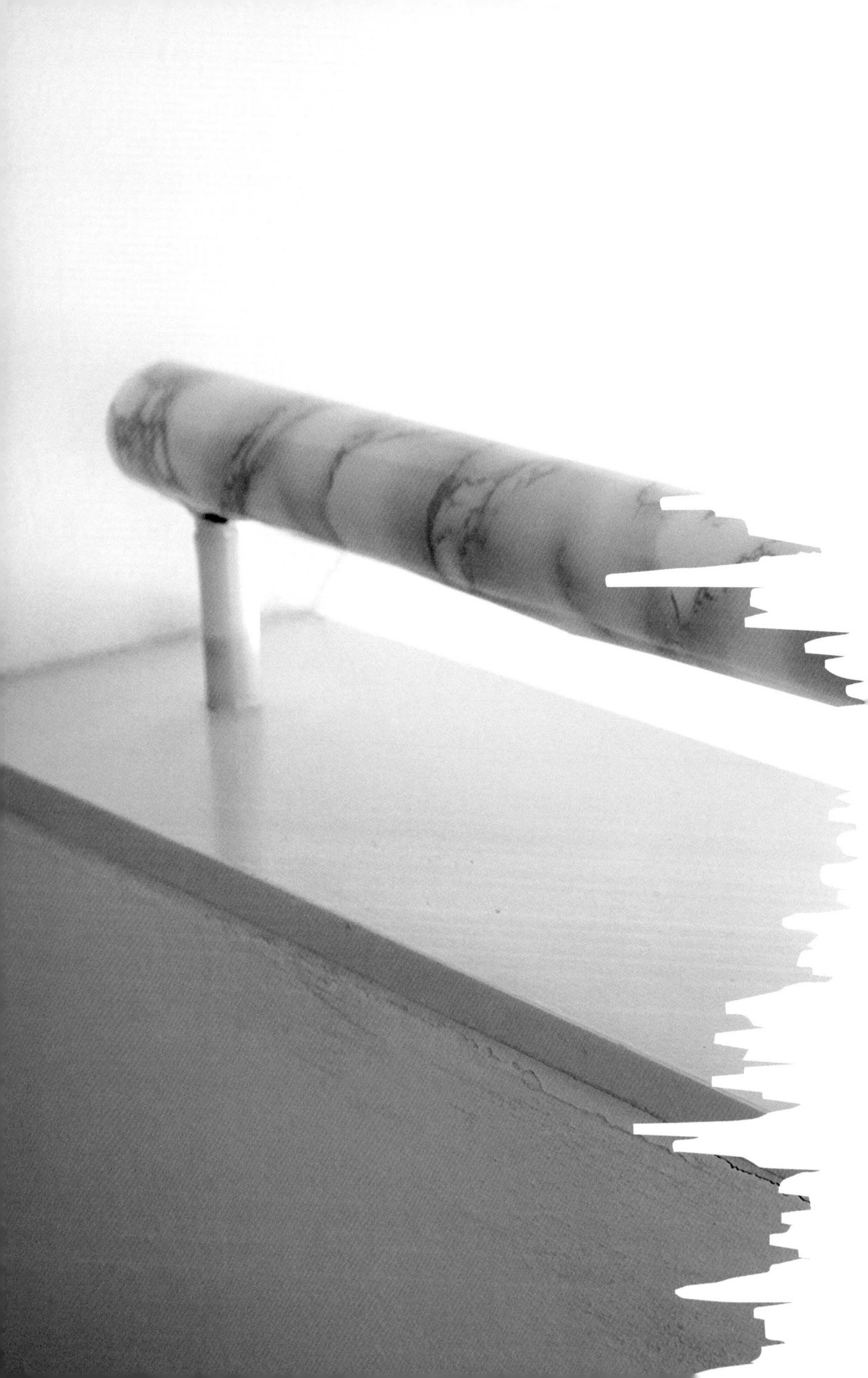

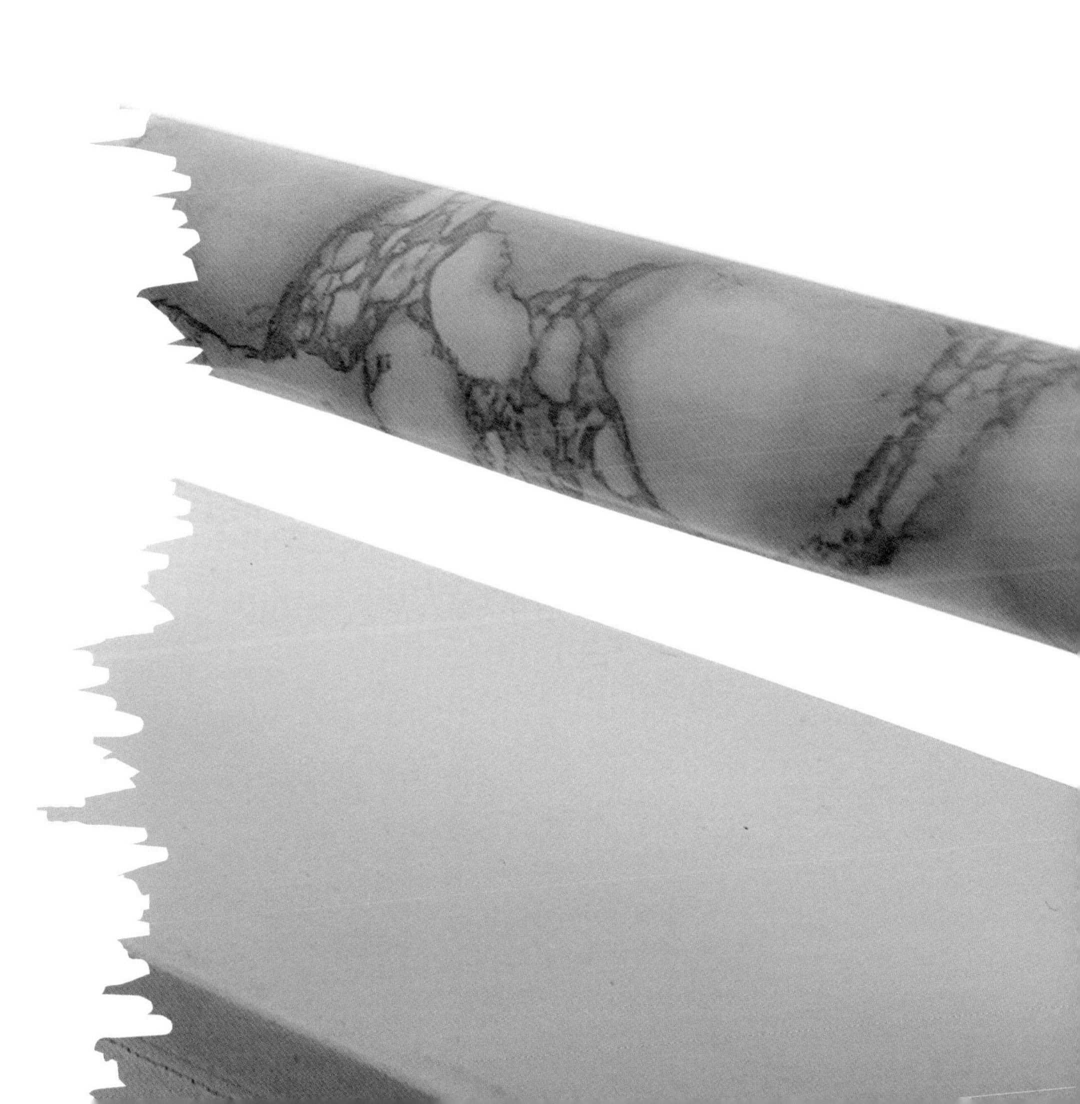

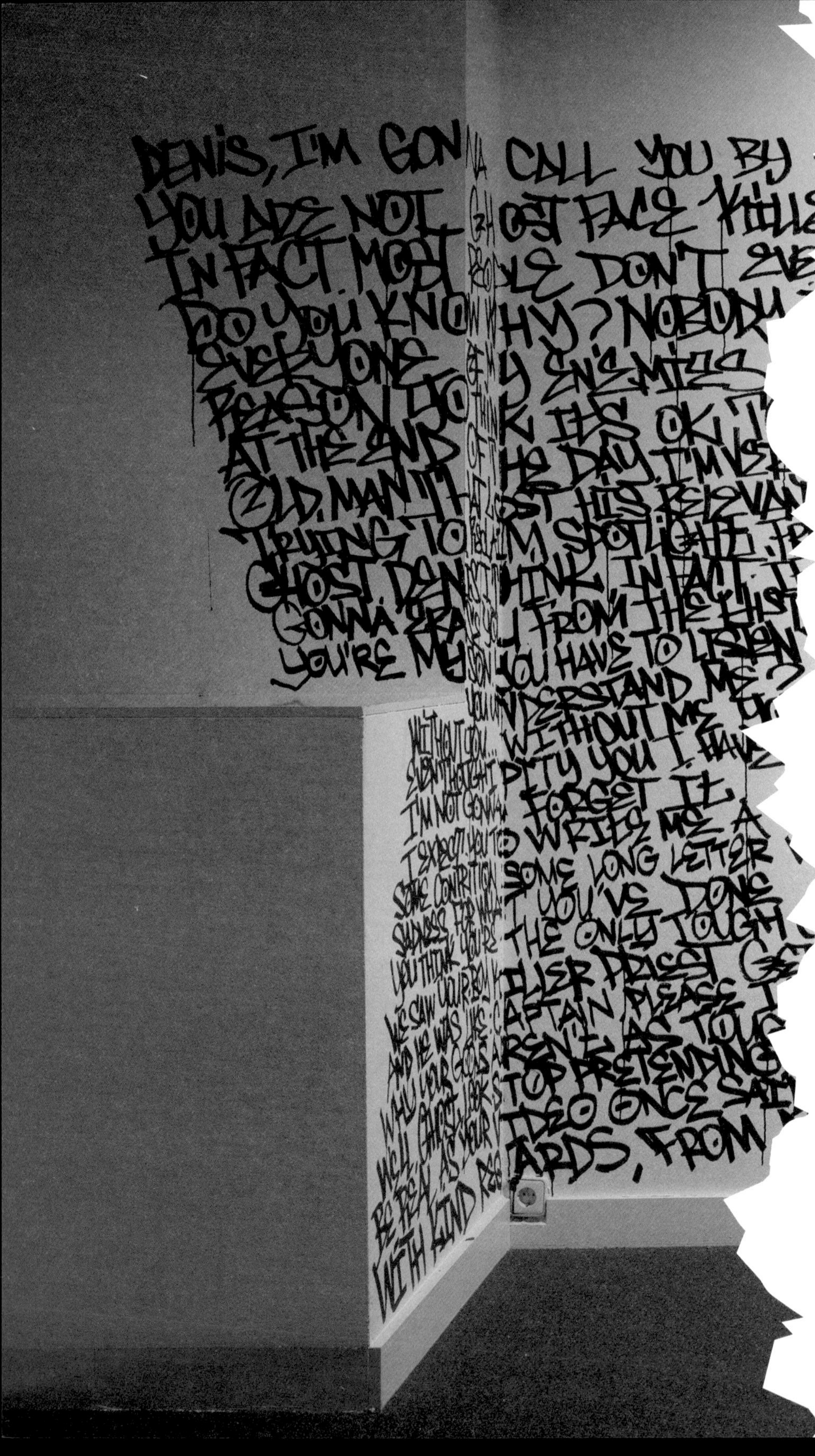

DENIS, I'M GONNA CALL YOU BY
YOU ARE NOT GHOST FACE KILLE
IN FACT MOST PEOPLE DON'T EVE
DO YOU KNOW WHY? NOBODY
EVERYONE MY ENEMIES
REASON HOW THINK IT'S OK
AT THE END OF THE DAY, I'M JUST
OLD MAN LOST HIS RELEVAN
TRYING TO M SPOTLIGHT
GHOST DON'T THINK. IN FACT
GONNA FROM THE LIST
YOU'RE MY YOU HAVE TO LISTEN
UNDERSTAND ME
WITHOUT YOU... WITHOUT ME
SILENT THOUGHT PITY YOU. I HAVE
I'M NOT GONNA FORGET IT
I EXPECT YOU TO WRITE ME A
SOME CONDITION SOME LONG LETTER
SADNESS FOR ALL YOU'VE DONE
YOU THINK YOU'RE THE ONLY TOUGH
WE SAW YOUR BOY ER PLACE, G
AND HE WAS HIS AIN PLEASE, I
WHO YOUR GOOD REN'T AS TOUG
WHO CAME STOP PRETENDING
WELL AS YOUR V IDEO ONCE SAI
ARDS, FROM
WITH KIND RE

MENT NAME.

SF WITH ME

ANONYMOUS, FOR WHATEVER
'S A BIG MISTAKE.
OU ARE AN OLD MAN.
G TO RECLAIM IT. AND YOU ARE
THAT IS NOT GONNA WORK.
ME DUMB SHIT AGAIN. I'M
RE GOING TO BE DONE.
YOUR BREAD.

PUNCH.
FROM THE HEART.
YOUR SORROW AND

SORRY, YOU DON'T KNOW US.

KIDS, WHY IS THAT?

LYING.
ER FUCKIN MENTION MY NAME AGAIN.
LF.

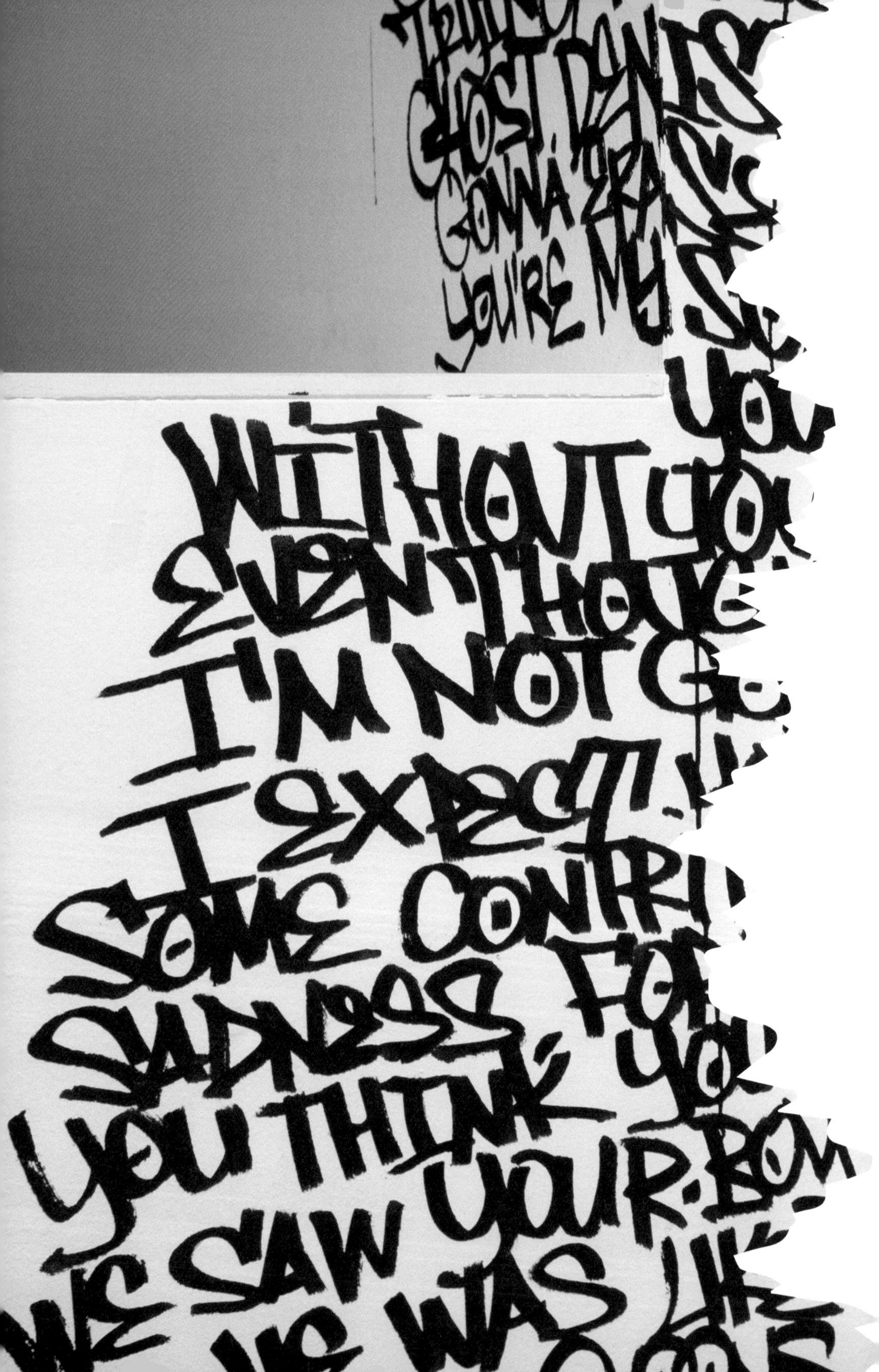
TRULY
GHOST DON'T
GONNA ERASE
YOU'RE MY
WITHOUT YOU
EVEN THOUG
I'M NOT G
I EXPECT
SOME CONTR
SADNESS FO
YOU THINK YO
WE SAW YOUR BOM
IT WAS LI

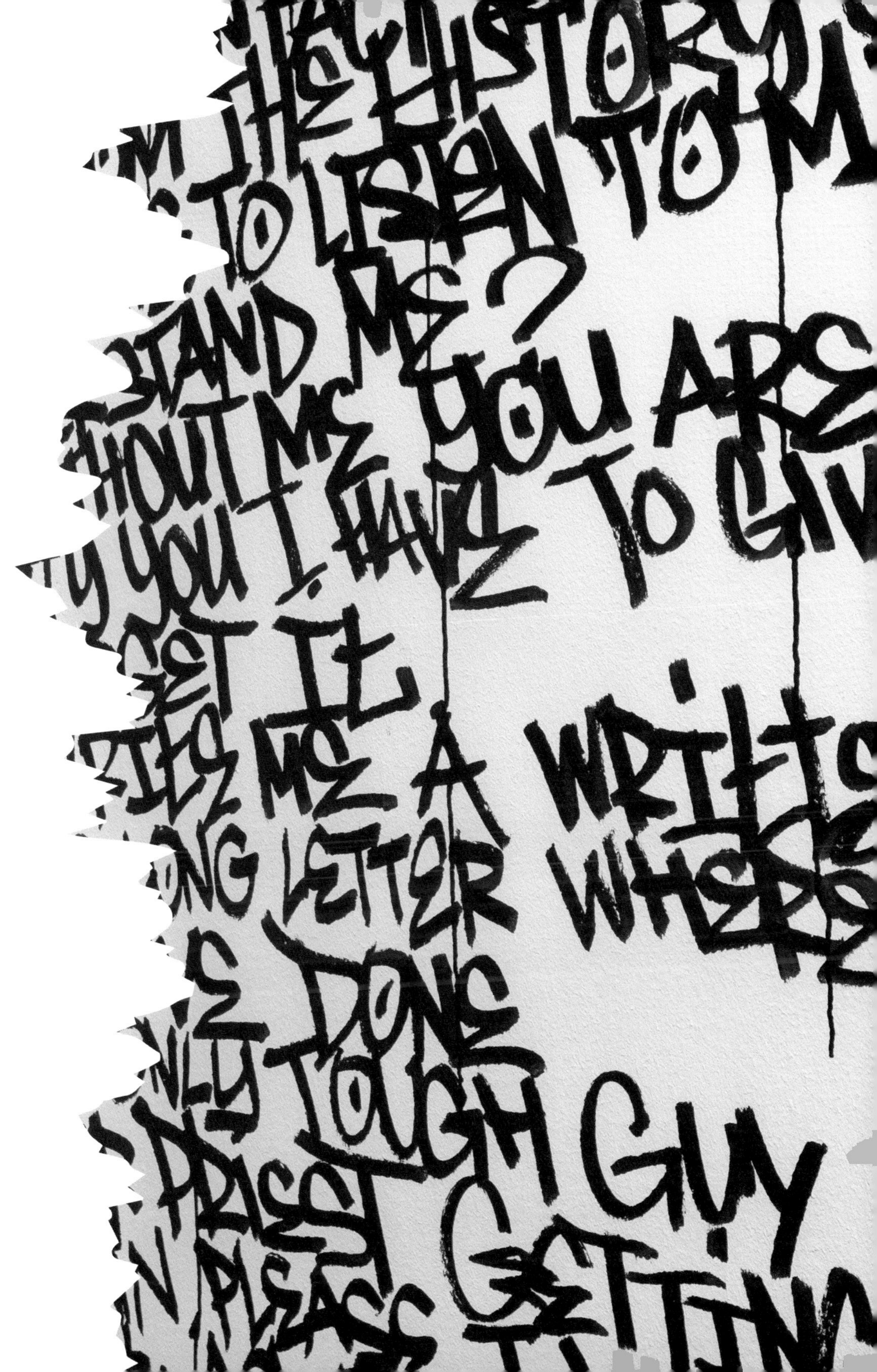
HISTORY
TO LISTEN TO M
STAND ME?
BOUT ME YOU ARE
Y YOU I HAVE TO GIV
GET IT
LIES ME A WRITTE
NG LETTER WHERE
DONE
LY TOUGH GUY
PRISSY GETTIN
PLEASE

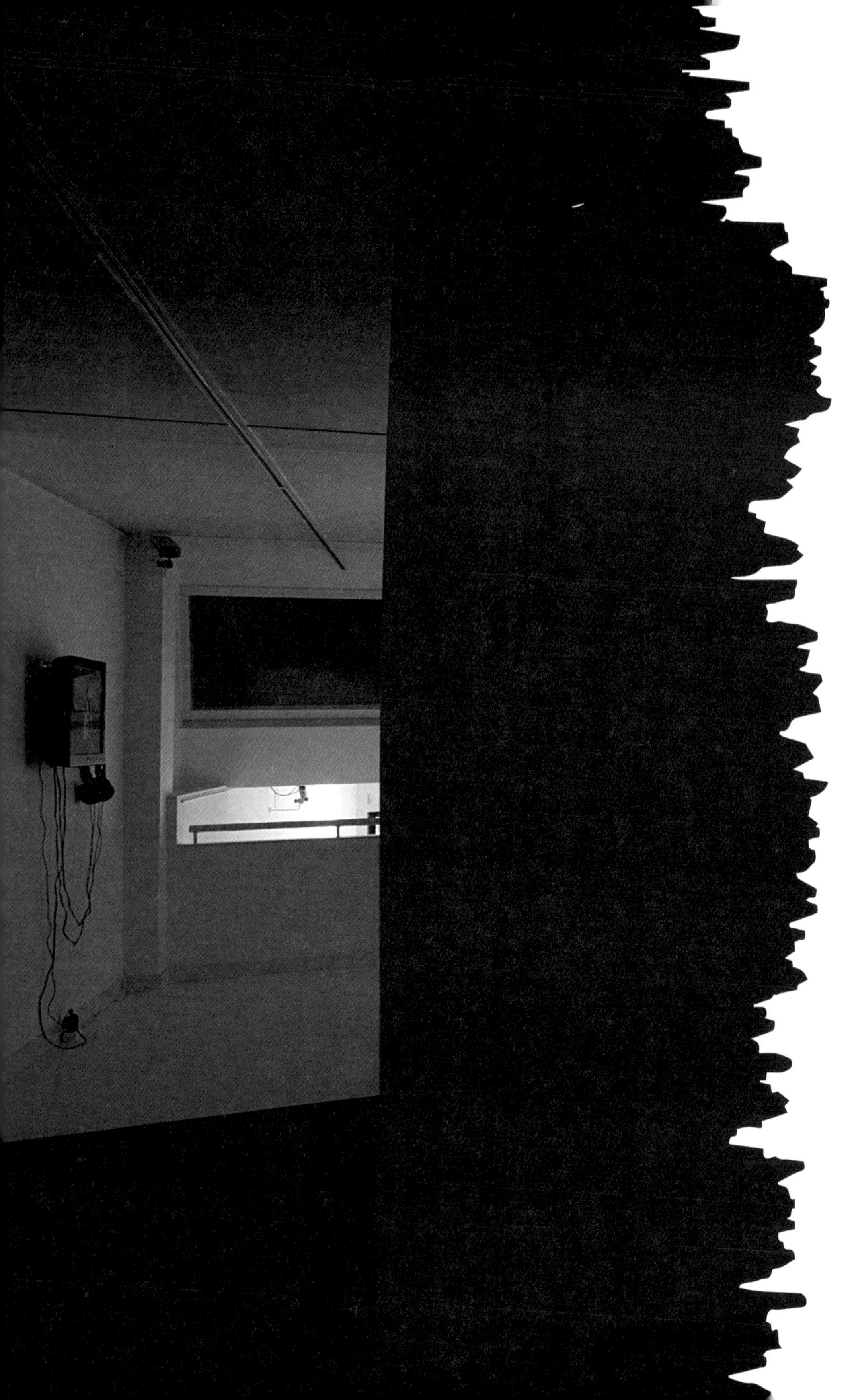

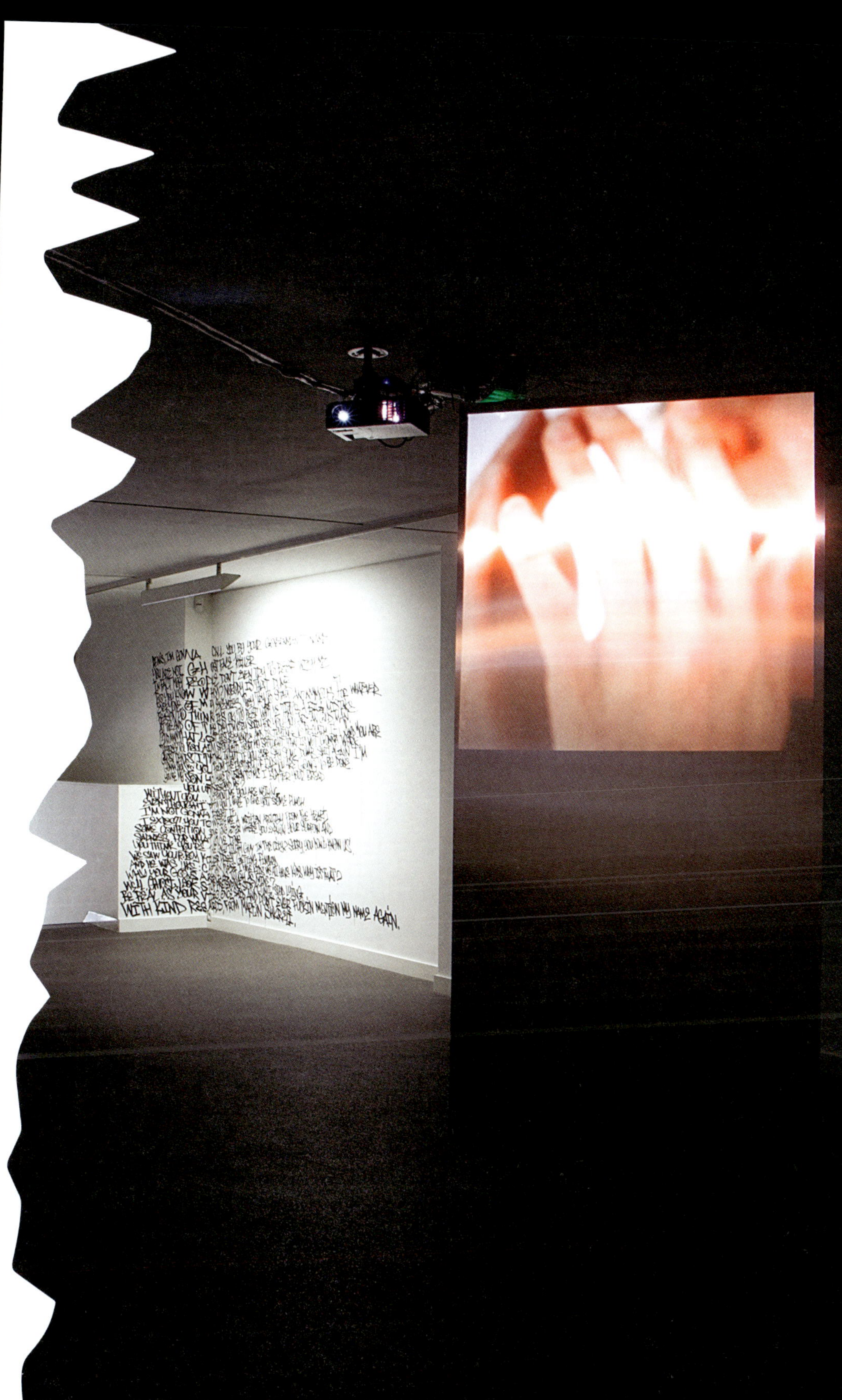

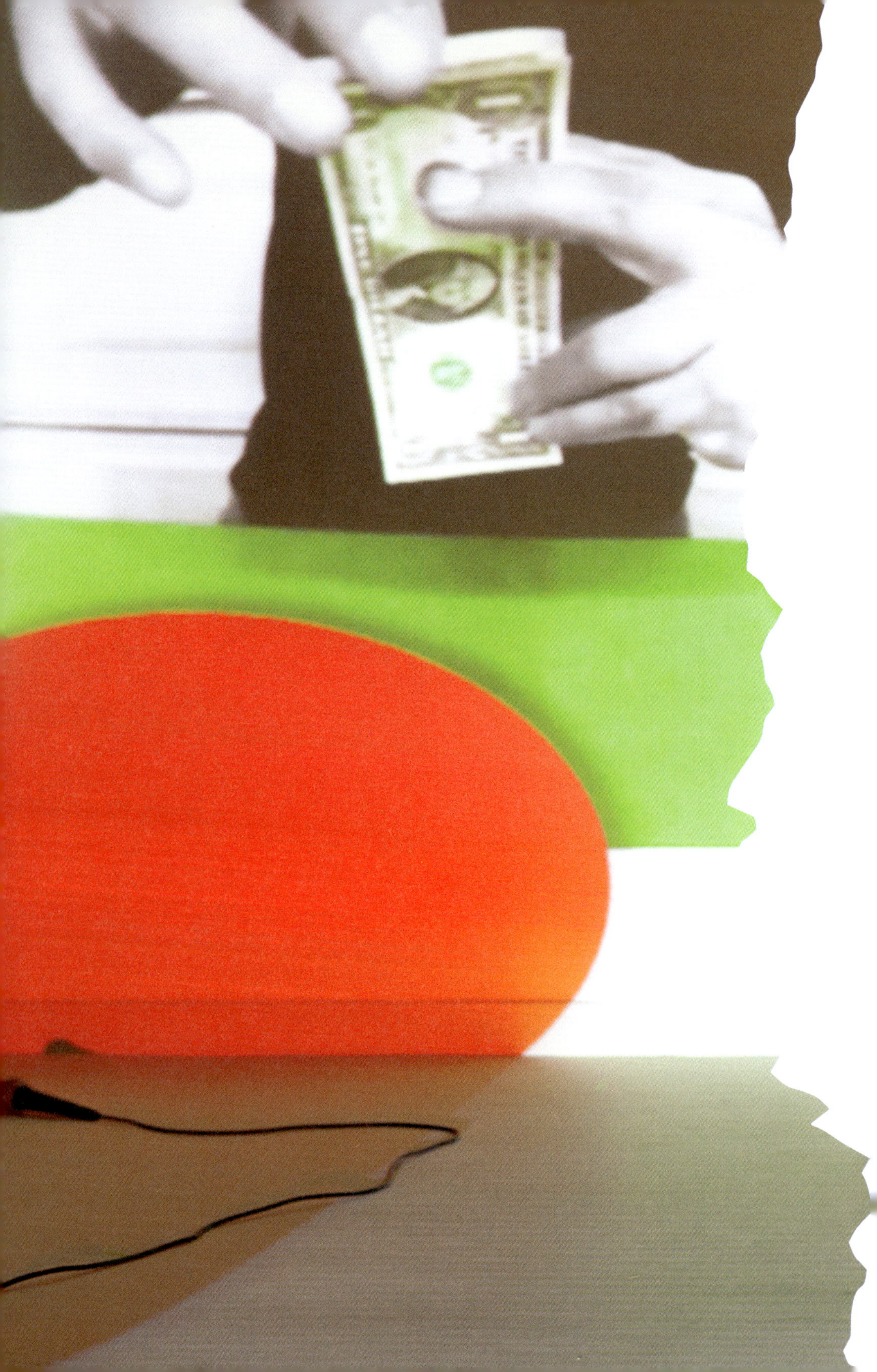

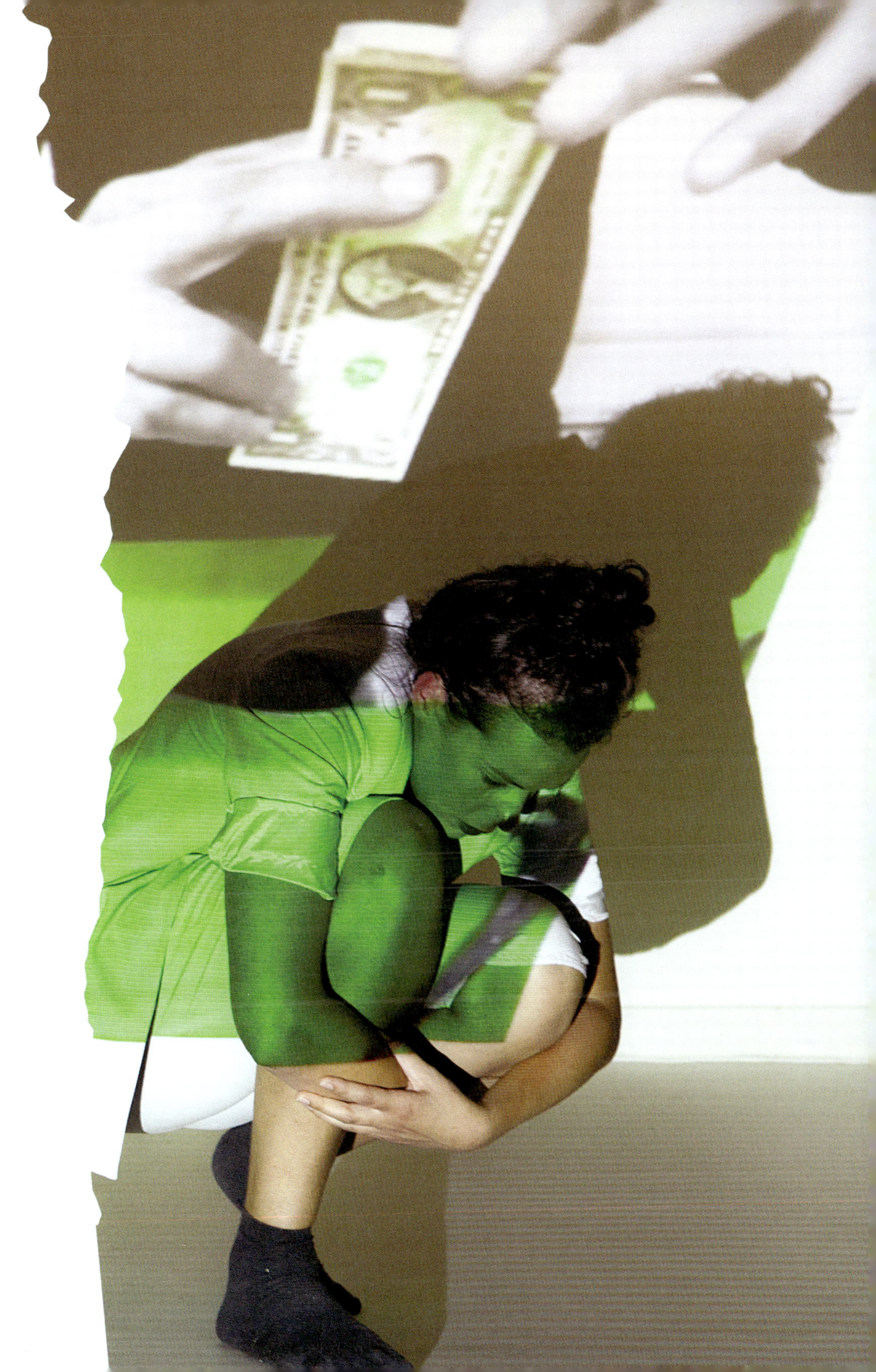

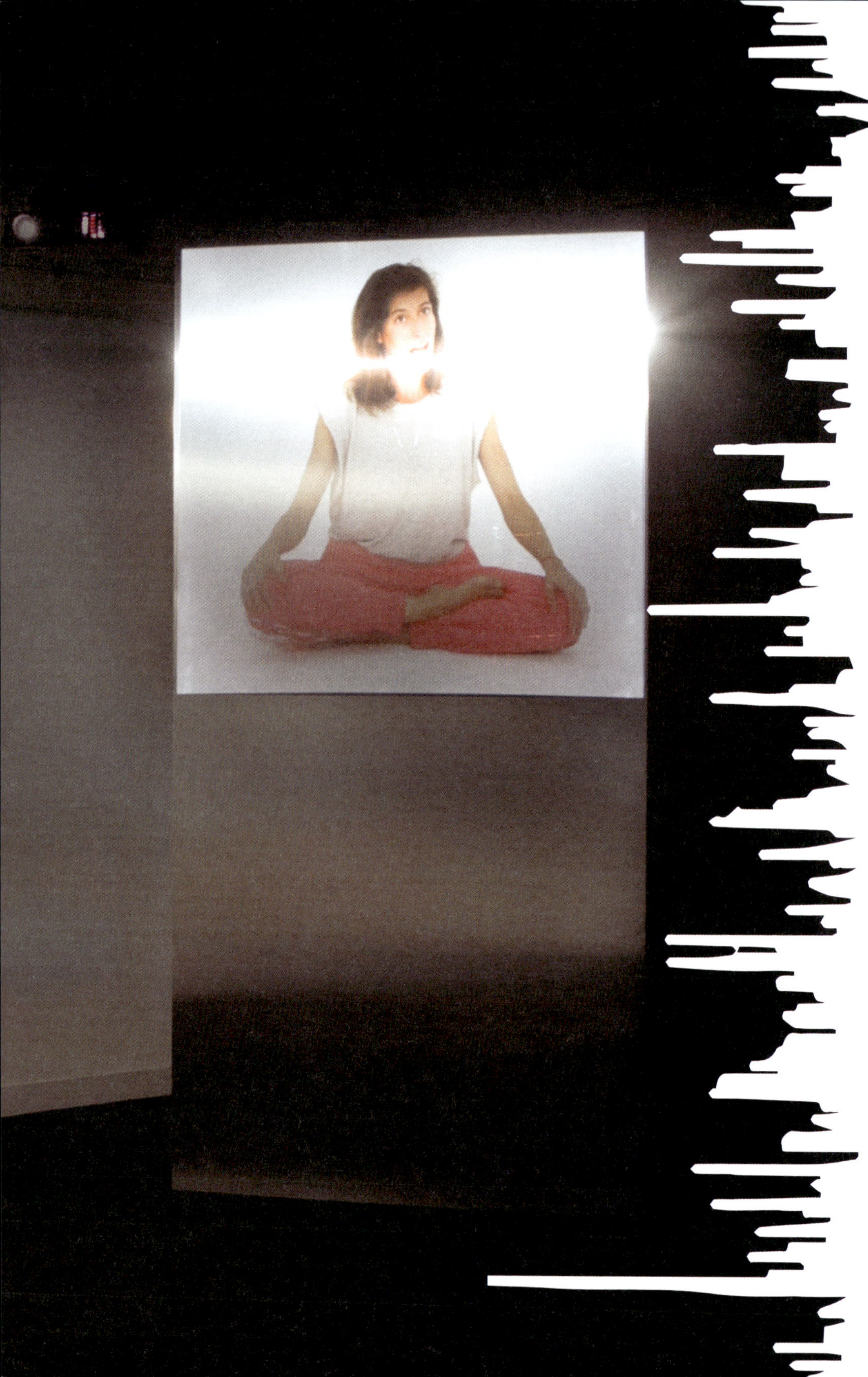

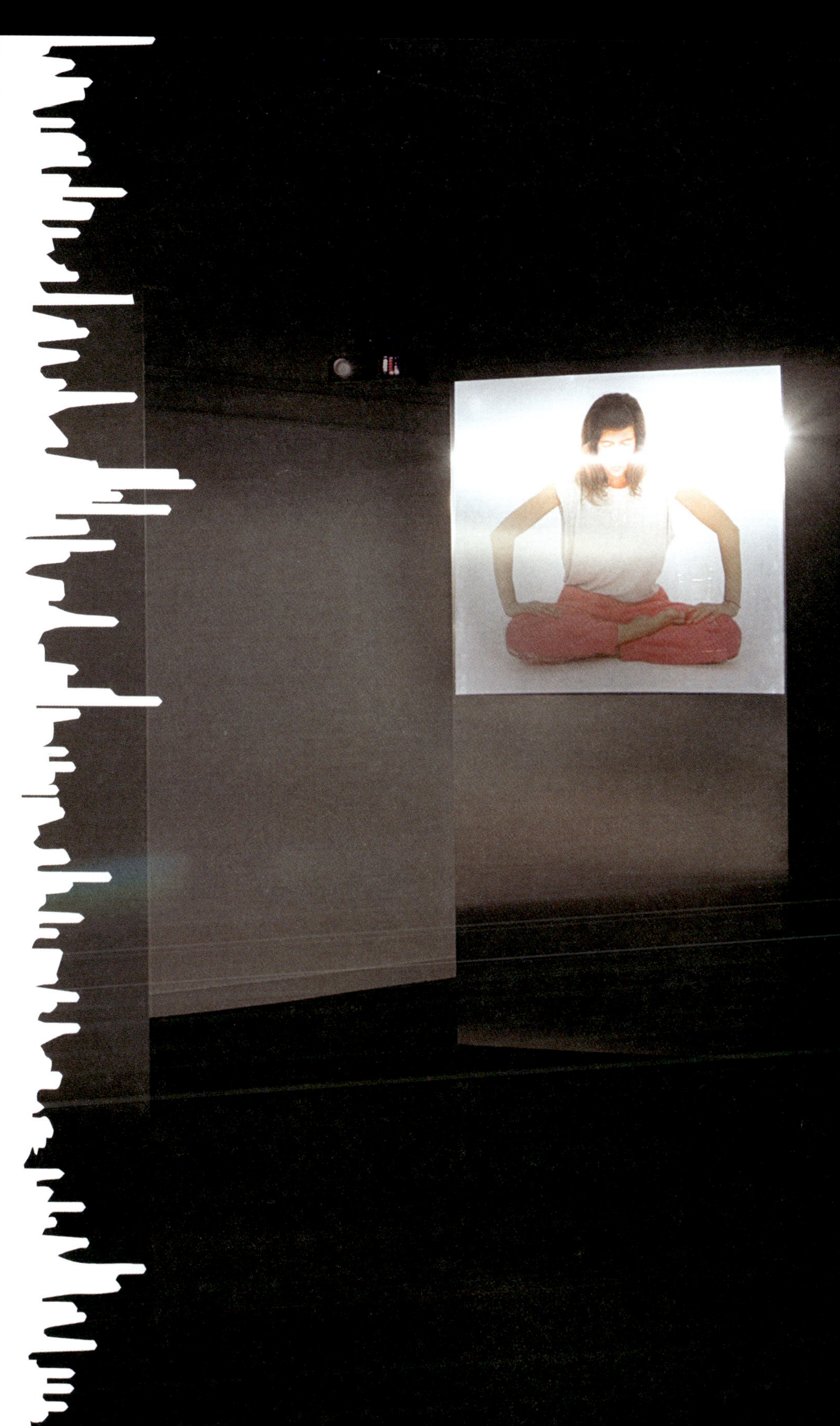

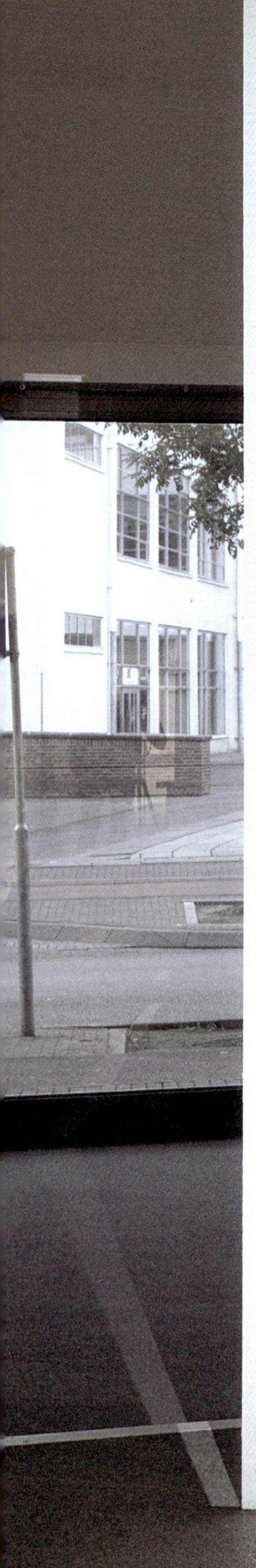

Het is alweer vier jaar
Aangezien u deze aarde hebben verlaten

Ik wil dat je weet,
Uw nalatenschap heeft waard.

In de grote stad Gary,
Waar je talent was geboren.

Uw jongensjaren was eng,
Je gevoel van eigenwaarde was gescheurd.

'Mijn vader is een groot genie "
Dat was je favoriete claim.

Maar waarom Sheild zo'n gemeenheid
En Protext hem van blaam?

Lelijke geruchten en praten
Zijn nog steeds verspreid over jou.

Waarom kunnen mensen niet zomaar
En dingen niet onwaar te zeggen?

Uw roem zal nooit stoppen

Hier zit ik, en ik werk,
Omdat het een vervelende kleine Turk,
Ik nauwelijks betaald en de uren zuigen,
Dus geef me een fucking

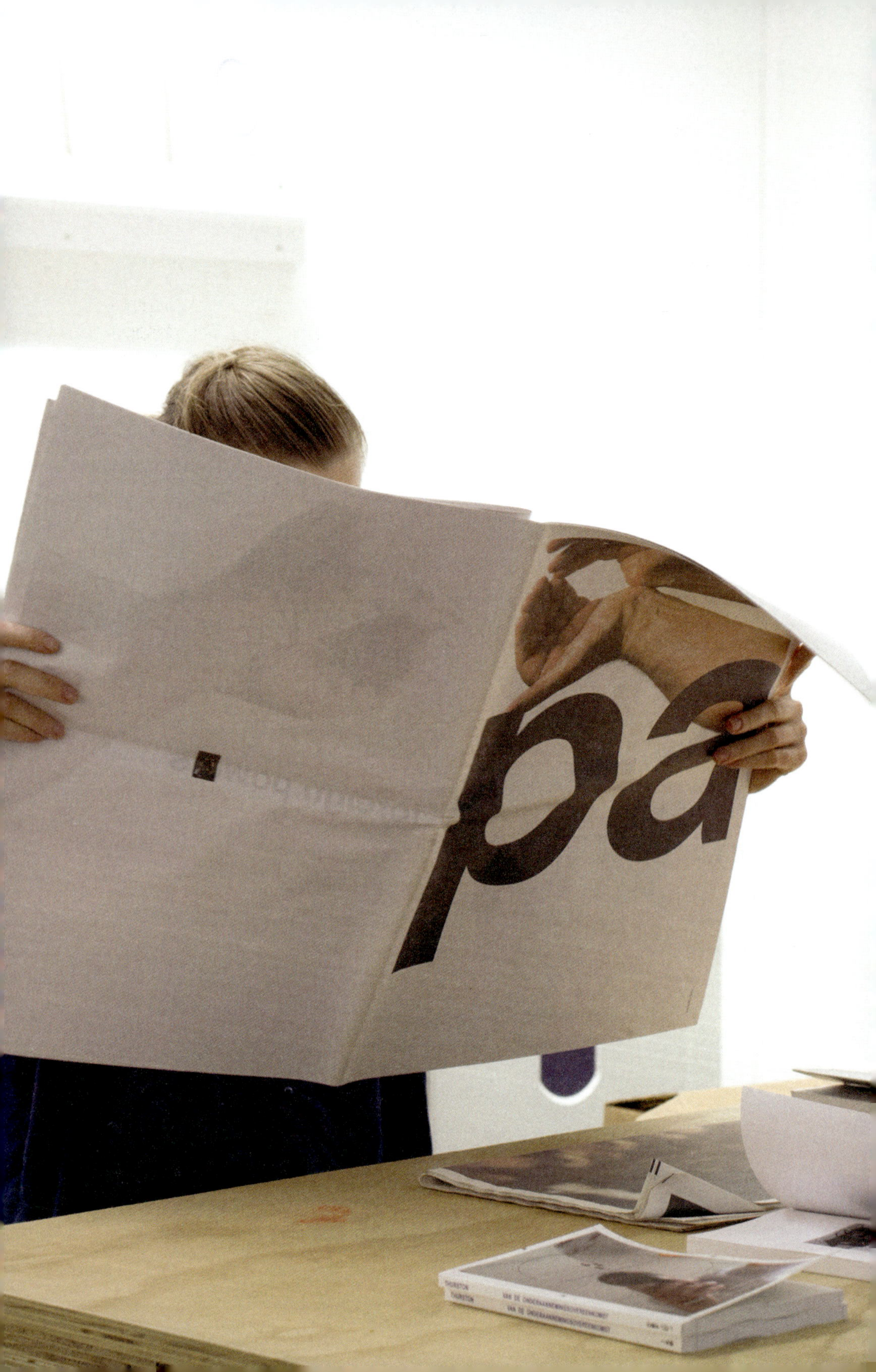

Dear Beloved-er,

Greetings of today and some days ahead. I have been thinking of you, in plural. Do you need a little help? Be honestly! In fact, we all need some help, despite our daily trip on a crowded bus towards an uncertain destiny without sincere compassion. Would you give up your seat to a fellow traveller when he falls flat? I think so. This is why I am speaking to you dear Belove-dest; when i first saw your profile today i already knew there was something inside of you, something I thought I will never find. Through the deceitful digital nature of a silken computer screen, your complexion glows like a fertilised field of budding cacti. The question is, are you lonely and bored too?

May I introduce myself to you: I am Dr. Helen Wong, owning a first degree in supreme international medicine services. Well done; you've just found the best kept secret to help build your own financial erection, whether you have a pole or not. Do not turn your blind ear to me: I tell you in confidence to WATCH OUT! as financial impotence can happen even to the most happiest of us, especially in spring. For the past year I have started to tilt over due to the burdensome accumulated wealth of 100 000 000 OOO %%0000 which has managed to keep me erect for years. I now need your dire help to stay upright and leave me of this financial burden. My secret is: drink this drink every morning and make an elephant out of your ant. For first time orders of my magic mixture which is GUARANTEED to cure your financial impotence, the price is only $5Ø00 incl. shipping. Once you start to see strong signs of financial erection I will transfer you the rest of my wealth in your local currency. But HURRY ASAPUP as there are many other candidates out there with equally glowing complexion, all depending on the lighting.

Did this message make you happy? I see.

TALK SOOŇ!

Sincerestly,
Dr. Helen Wong

Hello there,

I am Mrs Helen Wong from General Federal Bank of Kerching. You might not believe it, but please do.

Feeling down? Feeling tired? Feeling feelings? I know it all. I wish to contact you because you are about to make a big mistake in your life. I did a big mistake in my life, and now I am only half the person I once was. If you would you like to remain a whole, then listen to me. I have $ 500 000 000 000 000 000 000 000 000 000 000 000 000 000 000 000 000 000 which can make up for what you are missing. Build a house, make a plan, eat a cake and have it too, it's all possible from now on.

All you need to do is to donate a scarce crumb of $ 500 to the General Federal Bank of Kerching and you will feel whole again.

A whole is only a hole if there is nothing around it-

Yours definitely,
Mrs. Helen Wong

EPILOGUE

Thank you for inquiry.

**You are welcome to show The Financial Crisis. We charge a screening fee of
€2000 excluding all other expenses.**
**Investment Bank Flowerpots isn't available in its entirety of 20 buildings, but it's
possible to exhibit some buildings. It is a rather delicate work and we do have
certain requirements for the space, handling and transporting it.**

Please let me know how this sounds to you.

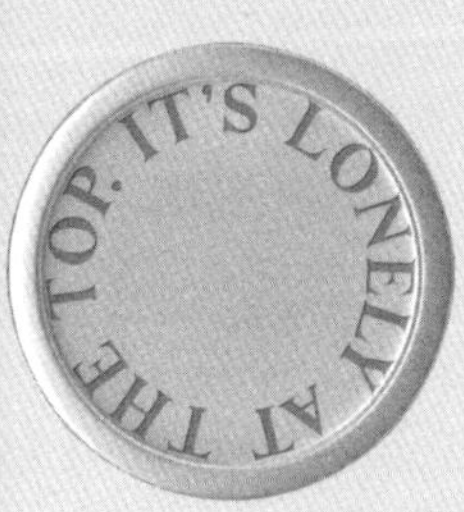

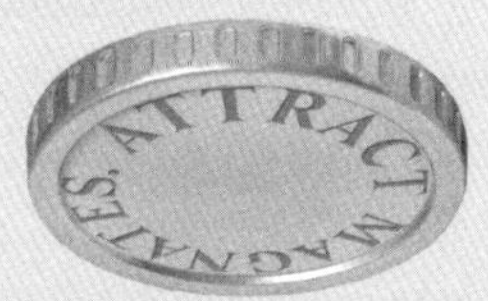

BIOGRAPHIES OF CONTRIBUTORS

MERCEDES AZPILICUETA

uses primarily voice and the affective quality of language as material for her work. In 2015-16 she was the resident of the Rijksakademie, Amsterdam. Azpilicueta earned an MFA from the Dutch Art Institute/ArtEZ, Arnhem and a BFA from Universidad Nacional de las Artes, Buenos Aires; where she also participated in the Artists' Program from Universidad Torcuato Di Tella.

KRIS DITTEL

is a curator and editor. Her curatorial work is framed by an interest in performativity, in relation to body and language, amd forms of mis/communication. Prior to her studies of Art and Heritage at the Maastricht University she graduated in Economics and Social Sciences at the Masaryk University in Brno, CZ. In 2013-14 Kris Dittel participated de Appel Curatorial Programme in Amsterdam.

ZACHARY FORMWALT

is an artist and filmmaker based in Amsterdam. He has presented solo projects at the Salon of the Museum of Contemporary Art Belgrade (2015); Stedelijk Museum Bureau Amsterdam (2014); Wexner Center for the Arts: The Box, Columbus, OH (2010); and Kunsthalle Basel (2009). In 2013, his film, *Unsupported Transit*, received a Tiger Award for Short Films at the International Film Festival Rotterdam.

SARA GIANNINI

is a semiotician engaged in curating, writing, and editing. Her research focuses on the liminality of language and representation resulting in collaborative projects with artists, curators and practitioners in other disciplines. Influenced by her background in theatre, her projects merge performativity and theory to probe the tropes and places of exhibition making.

MONIQUE HENDRIKSEN

graduated the Dutch Art Institute in Arnhem at AKV St. Joost in 's-Hertogenbosch and Breda. Prior to education in art she studied at the Business Economics at Fontys University Eindhoven and a Pre-Master in Philosophy at Tilburg University. This background informs her work where she aims to create a space to discuss and radicalize the entangled relations between art, theory and economics.

JAN HOEFT

often interrogates contemporary globalized society where he employs conceptual photography, video and public interventions. He studied at the Academy of Media Arts Cologne, the Academy of Fine Arts Karlsruhe and the University of Karlsruhe. In 2013-14 he was a resident at the Jan van Eyck Academy in Maastricht.

TORIL JOHANNESSEN

interdisciplinary practice engages with scientific themes through empirical
and theoretical investigation of the relationship between art and science. She
obtained her MA in Fine Arts from Bergen National Academy in 2008 and
attended the Mountain School of Arts in 2011. Her work has been widely
exhibited in galleries and institutions in Norway and internationally, as well
as at dOCUMENTA (13) (2012); The Istanbul Biennial (2012).

SAMI KHATIB

is a visiting professor of art theory at the American University of Beirut.
He was a researcher at the Theory Department of the Jan van Eyck Academie
Maastricht (2012) and earned his PhD degree in Media and Communication
Studies from Freie Universität Berlin (2013). His main research interests are in
Walter Benjamin Studies, Critical Theory, Psychoanalysis, Modern Continental
Philosophy, Art Theory, and German Studies.

HANNE LIPPARD

is a writer and visual artist living and working in Berlin. Lippard's practice
explores the voice as a medium. Her education in graphic design informs
how language can be visually powerful; her texts are visual, rhythmic, and
performative rather than purely informative.

ROBERTAS NARKUS

describes his practice as the "management of circumstance in an economy
of coincidence." He brings together the ordinary and the absurd to explore
notions of chance economics, hypothetical experiences and spiritual commerce.
Previously he exhibited at de XII Baltic Triennial, de Appel arts centre, Stroom
the Hague, Establiment de' en Face, Brussels.

ANTONIS PITTAS

creates context-sensitive installations, informed by architecture, art-historical
references, the performative aspects of installation art, and its social
dynamics. Amongst others he had solo exhibitions at De Nederlandsche Bank,
Amsterdam, Hessel Museum of Art & CSS Bard Galleries, Annandale,
New York (2012), Benaki Museum, Athens (2011), Van Abbe Museum,
Eindhoven (2011).

NICK THURSTON

is a writer who makes art works. He is the author or co-author of several
books, is co-editor of the publishing imprint Information As Material (York),
and his print and sculptural works are held in public and private collections
internationally. He has been an Associate and Visiting Lecturer at various art
academies in the UK and since 2012 joined the faculty of the School of Fine
Art, History of Art and Cultural Studies at the University of Leeds.

MCKENZIE WARK

is a writer and scholar, known for his writings on media theory, critical theory,
new media, and the Situationist International. He is author of A Hacker
Manifesto and Gamer Theory. He is a Professor of Culture and Media in
Liberal Studies at The New School for Social Research.

INDEX DETOUR

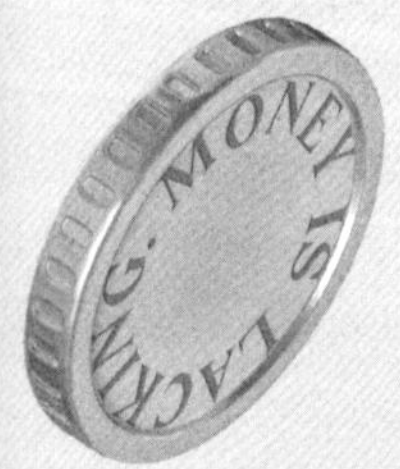

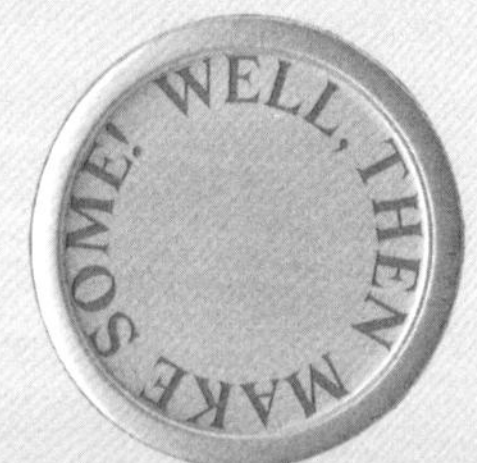

abstraction: commodity, 13, 26, 52, 54, 105; real, 12, 13, 22, 26, 42, 51-59; social, 42, 26

artificial intelligence 14, 103-106

artificial artificial intelligence 103-106

Austrian School of Economics 29

Automated Trading System (ATS) 34

balance: 15, 27, 64-65; counter, 24

bank: 16, 28, 65, 98; German, 75; French, 68; General Federal of Kerching, 27, 47, 86-87, 116, 150

banker 31

Benjamin, Walter 12, 22, 26, 54, 56, 59

Beyoncé 40

Bible 21, 23, 24, 28

spambot 15

capital: 11-13, 42-43, 52-57, 68, 75, 98; linguistic, 35

Capital 49-51, 66, 98

capitalism: 12, 13, 14, 25, 26, 30, 51, 89-96; computational, 14,106; cognitive, 30, 89, 91; financial, 28; the mantra of 12; religious structure of, 12; mythology of, 21; history of, 24, 50

coin 16, 40, 86

commodity: 16, 28, 49, 54, 56, 99; abstraction, 15, 50, 52, 54; exchange, 15, 50, 57; form, 90, 92, 96; language, 23

Crédit Mobilier 68

economy: 11, 22, 24, 30, 54, 92; of debt, 59; on demand, 104; language, 35; is spinning, 11-16; of time, 54; political, 13, 42, 65-66, 98

exchange: 11, 15, 23, 29, 33, 39-40, 43, 50, 52, 77; commodity, 13, 50, 53, 57; medium of, 65; exchange value, 29-30, 49, 90, 92

Federal Reserve 30

fetishism: 43; of capital, 49, 58

fiction: 14-15, 43, 58; science, 57, 100

glossolalia 32

God 22-32, 42

hacker class 97-99

investment 33-34, 68

labour: 13, 30, 49, 51-57; abstract, 13, 49-59; artificial, 104; exploited, 14; manual, 38

language: 11-16, 21-23, 29-33, 89-94, 100, 103; body, 40; of economics and finance, 11, 30, 32; religious, 12; of revolution, 14

Latin Monetary Union 74-75

magic 26, 31-32, 91

Marx, Karl 13, 21, 28-29, 30, 49-55, 58, 63-69, 90, 93-96, 98, 100

Messianic 28, 59, 89, 93

miracle 25, 28, 31, 35

neoliberal 67, 77-78, 89, 91, 94

PIGS 68

performance: 13, 16, 38, 103-105; linguistic, 21; vocal, 31

poetry : 93, 100, 102-107; visual, 12

production: 16, 29-31, 42, 50-56, 66, 74, 89-98, 102-105; modes of, 42, 89, 98

prudence 13, 78

religion 11, 26, 31, 56

Schäuble, Wolfgang 13, 61-63, 67-71, 76-78

sensuous supra-sensuous 49, 57-59

sentiment analysis 34

semiotic 21, 23, 25, 28-30, 99

sign: 30; linguistic, 29

signifier 22-25, 42, 92

signified 22-25, 42, 92

Sohn-Rethel, Alfred 13, 40, 43, 50, 53

spambot 15

spinning: 11-16, 102; wheel, 51-52, 56

sponsor 62, 68, 70

subcontract 14, 102-104, 106-107

time: 40, 50-57, 86, 97; labour 51-54; language and, 22; infinite, 39; of the production process, 50-55, 90-91; of capital, 52, 55, 56-57, 59; part- 99

translation 23, 100, 102, 104, 106

value: 22, 33-34, 50-58, 74-75, 97, 102, 105; exchange, 29-30, 49, 90, 92; linguistic, 29; surplus, 13, 56-57, 90; spinning, 52; postal, 59; use, 90, 92

vampire 54-55, 57

vectoralist class 97-99

Wong, Helen 15, 27, 47, 86-87, 116, 149-150

zombie 13, 56-57

LIST OF WORKS IN THE EXHIBITION

Mercedes Azpilicueta
GEOMETRIC DANCER DOESN'T BELIEVE IN LOVE,
FINDS ASPIRATION AND ECSTASY IN SPIRALS
synchronized looped video projections
with sound 20'30", aluminum sheets
2015

Zachary Formwalt
KRITIK DER POLITIK UND NATIONALÖKONOMIE
photograph 35 x 30 cm
2009

Monique Hendriksen
ON NATURE
HD video, colour, sound, 9'20"
2016

Monique Hendriksen
DELUSIONAL CAUSE
performance with HD video projection and sound
2015–ongoing

Jan Hoeft
EXIT STRATEGIES
HD video, colour, sound, 6'30" on loop
2014

Toril Johannessen
WORDS AND YEARS—PHYSICAL AND ECONOMIC
EXPANSION AND RECESSION; CRISIS IN NATURE
AND SCIENCE; LOGIC AND LOVE IN ART
silkscreen prints, 76 x 56 cm
2010

Hanne Lippard
THE SSECRET TO SSUCCESS ISS IN THE SS-ESS
voice installation, 7'14"
2014

Hanne Lippard
I AM MRS HELEN WONG, WE NEED TO
DISCUSS AS PROMISED
performance
2015

Robertas Narkus
CONTRACT
text on wall,
dimensions variable
2016

Antonis Pittas
DONKEY
5 steel structures with neon light,
each 139 x 75 x 44 cm
2015–16

Antonis Pittas
CLIP (UNTITLED)
steel and marble, photographic images,
various dimensions
2015

Nick Thurston
VAN DE ONDERAANNEMING OF,
PRINCIPLES OF POETIC RIGHT
data projection, 30', looped
2016

Nick Thurston
VAN DE ONDERAANNEMINGSOVEREENKOMST,
OF BEGINSELEN VAN POËTISCHE RECHT
limited edition publication, Onomatopee 132.1
2016

Onomatopee 132
Research project

THE ECONOMY IS SPINNING

ISBN 978-94-91677-61-8

Published in conjunction with
the exhibition The Economy
is Spinning, taking place at
Onomatopee between
9th June and 17th July, 2016.

EDITOR
Kris Dittel

CONTRIBUTING AUTHORS
Mercedes Azpilicueta
Zachary Formwalt
Sara Giannini
Monique Hendriksen
Jan Hoeft
Sami Khatib
Hanne Lippard
Toril Johannessen
Robertas Narkus
Antonis Pittas
Nick Thurston
McKenzie Wark

GRAPHIC DESIGN
Rafaela Dražić

IMAGE COURTESY
Exhibition and performance
photography courtesy of
Onomatopee. All other images
appear courtesy of the respective
artists unless otherwise stated.
Poster: courtesy Toril Johannessen
and OSL contemporary. Page 19
photo by Javier Agustín Rojas/
SlyZmud, courtesy of Mercedes
Azpilicueta. Pages 80–85:
courtesy of Antonis Pittas and
Annet Gelink Gallery.

PROOFREADING
Will Pollard

PRINTED AT
Kerschoffset Zagreb d.o.o.

EDITION OF
1200

THANK YOU
All artists and contributors for
their generosity and engagement,
the team of Onomatopee:
Freek Lomme, Pernilla Ellens and
Guus van der Velden, furthermore
Rafaela Dražić for the thoughtful
design, Will Pollard for poetic
licensing, and Anna Dasović.

Made possible thanks to
the generous support of the
Mondriaan Fonds and the
municipality of Eindhoven.

DISTRIBUTION
Onomatopee
shop@onomatopee.net
www.onomatopee.net

MARKETS LOOSE FAITH.

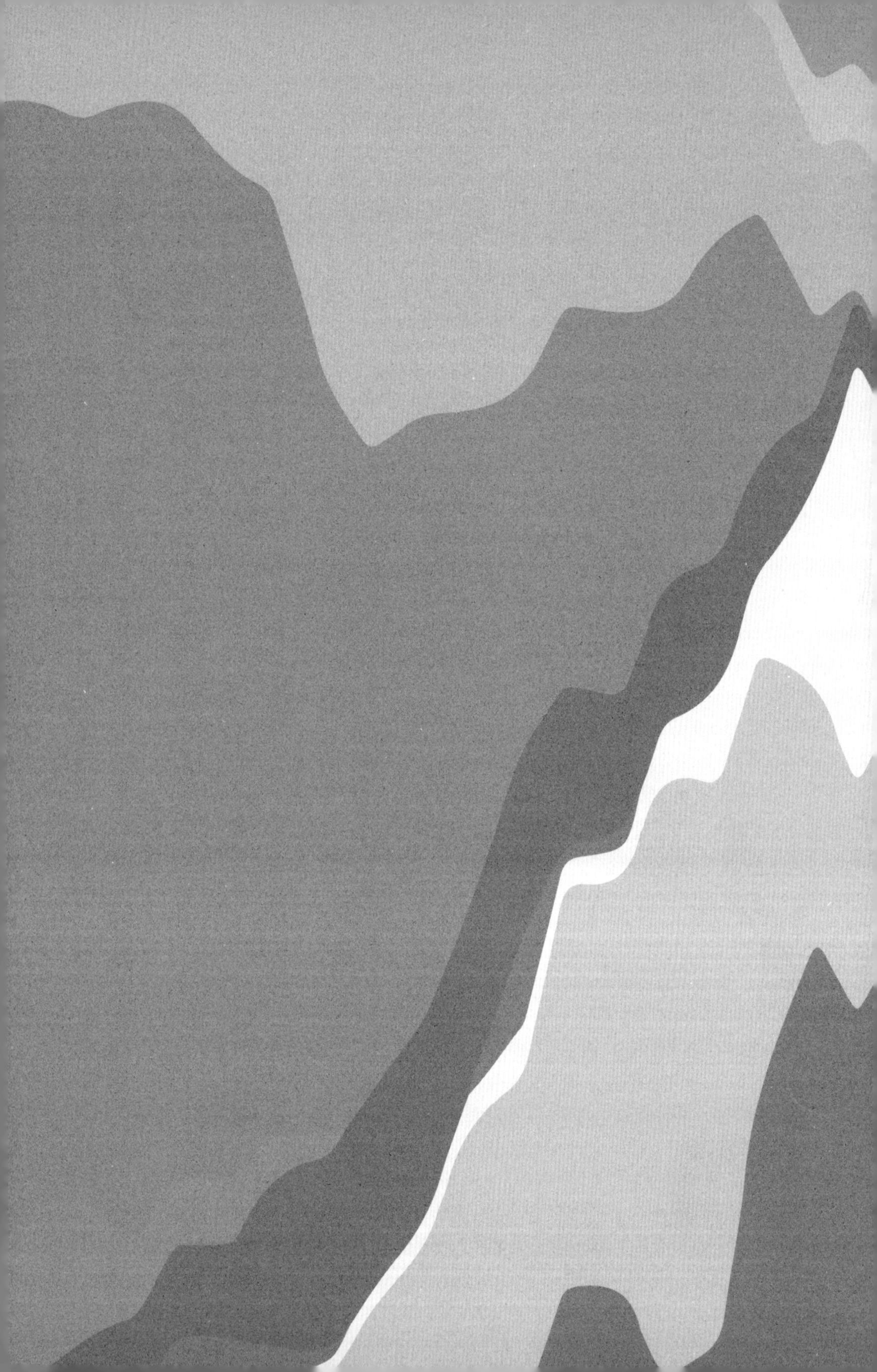